OUR PURPOSE IS LOVE

our purpose is

love

the Wesleyan way to be the church

David N. Field

Abingdon Press / Nashville

OUR PURPOSE IS LOVE:
THE WESLEYAN WAY TO BE THE CHURCH

Library of Congress Cataloging-in-Publication has been requested.

ISBN 978-1-5018-6867-2

Scripture quotations unless noted otherwise are taken from the Common English Bible, copyright 2011. Used by permission. All rights reserved.

Scripture quotations marked (NRSV) are taken from the New Revised Standard Version Bible, copyright © 1989 National Council of the Churches of Christ in the United States of America. Used by permission. All rights reserved worldwide. http://nrsvbibles.org/

18 19 20 21 22 23 24 25 26 27—10 9 8 7 6 5 4 3 2 1

MANUFACTURED in the UNITED STATES of AMERICA

To Caroline, Carlo, and Ernst

In gratefulness for
their love, support, and encouragement—
this book would not have happened without them.

CONTENTS

1

WHY IS LOVE THE ANSWER?

God created humanity in God's own image,
  in the divine image God created them,
    male and female God created them. (Gen 1:27)

The person who doesn't love does not know God, because God is
love. (1 John 4:8)

Tension, polarization, and conflict are part of our daily experience. Television news shows bring reports and images of international and national conflicts into our living rooms. Political debates quickly degenerate into name-calling, disparagement, and verbal abuse. Differences of political opinion among friends, neighbors, and colleagues quickly intensify into personal conflicts. Social media has become a means of trading insults, denigrating others, reinforcing stereotypes, and intensifying conflicts. Even in our churches, it seems that there is no longer a place for sincere disagreement. People with differing political, social, or theological viewpoints are quickly demonized. As Christians, we know we are supposed to love one another, but even that mandate has come to mean different things to different people. Some interpret love as being in agreement with one's neighbor rather than acting toward one's neighbor in a way that mirrors the compassionate, grace-giving heart of God. The questions we are confronted with are: "What does it mean to love God and neighbor today—in both the world and the church—and why is this the answer to the conflict that divides and polarizes us?" This book is a response to these questions; it examines John Wesley's understanding of God's love and asks how we are to embody it in the church and the world today.

To begin, let's go back to the beginning.

Why Did God Create Human Beings?

Understanding why God created human beings and how we fit into God's purpose in the world is foundational to understanding why love is the answer for not only our time but all time. Genesis 1:27 tells us that we were created in the image of God. Christian thinkers through the centuries have wrestled with the question of what this means and have come up with an array of answers. What *does* it mean to be created in God's image?

Let's consider Gen 1:27 through the lens of biblical scholarship, as well as the theology of the founder of Methodism, John Wesley.

A Biblical Understanding

Contemporary biblical scholars have brought greater clarity to the question of what it means to be created in the image of God by focusing on what would have come into the minds of the ancient

Israelites when they heard the words of Gen 1:27. In the ancient cultural and religious context, the concept of the image of a god could refer to a statue or picture that represented the god and was the focus of worship; or to kings and priests who acted on behalf of the god and were to be served and obeyed. The stone carving of a god was designed to portray the character of the god, while the kings and priests were understood to represent the interests of the gods in the society. The author of Gen 1 uses these common ideas in a new way, describing not stone carvings or kings and priests, but all human beings. So, when the ancient Israelites heard this phrase, they understood it to mean that all human beings were created to portray the character of Israel's God and represent God's interests in the world. This means that, as human beings, we have the privilege and responsibility of being God's representatives in the world. Our character, lifestyle, and actions should be portraits of who God is and what God is doing in the world.

In the next chapter of Genesis, we read, "The LORD God took the human and settled him in the garden of Eden to farm it and to take care of it" (Gen 2:15). It's noteworthy that the words translated "farm it" and "take care of it" have not only agricultural meaning, but also are used in religious contexts, referring to the service of priests and Levites in the Tabernacle. In fact, many of the images used to describe the garden of Eden are also related to symbols from the Tabernacle; interestingly, creation stories from Israel's neighbors often concluded with the establishment of a temple or sanctuary. Seen in this context, it's as if human beings are being portrayed not merely as farmers but as priests who are the mediators of God's blessing to the earth and its inhabitants.

What does this have to do with our understanding of what it means to be created in the image of God? God created human beings to reflect God's character, to represent God's interests, and in so doing to be a source of blessing for the earth. This raises two other questions we will explore in this chapter: *Who is God?* and *What is God like?*

A Wesleyan Understanding

The name *Methodist* goes back to the time when John Wesley and some of his friends at Oxford University formed a sort of club. They met regularly and tried to order their lives according to clear rules; they studied the Bible; attended Communion at least once a week; and sought practical ways to meet the needs of the poor, the uneducated, prisoners, and others on the margins of society. They were prepared to sacrifice not only their material possessions but also their reputations for those in need. To self-sacrificially care for the needy was not merely an obligation; it was, for them, a way of expressing the character of God revealed in Jesus Christ. They were trying to imitate Christ in the world. This commitment to imitating Christ had a deeper foundation; in following Christ as the "image of the invisible God" (Col 1:15), we embody the image of God in the world. As Wesley developed his understanding of what it meant to imitate Christ in the world, he returned again and again to the description of humanity being created in the image of God in Gen 1:27. This became a central theme in his theology. He understood the "image of God" as having three dimensions: (1) the *natural* image, which is our ability to think, understand, and make responsible decisions; (2) the *political* image, which is our calling to represent God in the world by lovingly and caringly ruling over creation; (3) and the *moral* image, which refers to our calling to embody the moral character of God. In other words, we are to reflect God's character on the earth. Wesley's understanding of the moral image of God—the nature of God—was shaped by the grand story of God's interaction with humanity described in the Bible and best defined by the life, death, and resurrection of Jesus Christ.

Another concept Wesley used to describe the unique place that human beings have in God's purposes in the world is the image of a *steward*. A steward is a servant entrusted with responsibility for the administration, well-being, and flourishing of the master's property and resources, and the steward must give an accounting to the master. Though *stewardship* has become a popular term in contemporary reflections on the care of creation, Wesley's understanding is more focused: all that we possess belongs to God, and so we are stewards of all that we are and have. Our calling, then, is to use all of who we are and what we have in promoting or helping God's purposes to flourish in the world. This brings us back again to the questions: *Who is God?* and *What is God like?*

Who Is God? and What Is God Like?

In the Bible, we read many descriptions of the character of God. In Exod 34:6, God describes God's own character as "compassionate and merciful, / very patient, / full of great loyalty and faithfulness." Throughout the Old Testament, we find references to these aspects of God's character as defining who God is and how God acts. For example, the author of Ps 86:15 motivates his cry for help from God by stating:

> But you, my Lord,
> are a God of compassion and mercy;
> you are very patient and full of faithful love.

Perhaps the most striking reference is found in Jonah's complaint to God after God refuses to punish Nineveh: "Come on, LORD! Wasn't this precisely my point when I was back in my own land? This is why I fled to Tarshish earlier! I know that you are a merciful and compassionate God, very patient, full of faithful love, and willing not to destroy" (Jonah 4:2).

For Christians, God is most fully revealed in the life, teaching, crucifixion, and resurrection of Jesus—the embodiment of God's compassion, mercy, faithfulness, and love. Jesus' parables declare the love of God, particularly to those who are excluded and rejected; and his miracles are expressions of compassion for the sick and suffering. When Jesus calls his followers to imitate God, he focuses on God's unconditional love for all humankind (Matt 5:43-48). The New Testament writers consistently describe the crucifixion as the expression of self-sacrificial love that makes the ultimate sacrifice to overcome sin and evil. It is on the cross that the character of God is most profoundly revealed. First John 4:8 can thus sum up God's character with the simple statement, "God is love."

John Wesley drew upon these and other biblical descriptions of God in his own writings about the nature of God, including these excerpts:

> Love existed from eternity, in God, the great ocean of love.[1]

> God is often styled holy, righteous, wise; but not holiness, righteousness, or wisdom in the abstract; as he is said to be love: intimating that this is his darling, his reigning attribute; the attribute that sheds an amiable glory on all his other perfections.[2]

John's brother, Charles, penned these words about God's nature in his hymn "Come, O Thou Traveler Unknown":

Pure Universal Love Thou art:

To me, to all, thy bowels move—
Thy nature, and thy name, is LOVE.[3]

The second line of this stanza seems rather strange to us today, but in eighteenth-century English, the bowels were metaphorically used to describe kindness, tenderness, compassion, and pity.

What difference does this make? What we understand as the central dynamic of the character of God will shape how we think about other characteristics or descriptions of God and God's actions. We will come up with a very different understanding of God if, for example, we put *sovereignty* and *glory* at the center of our description of God's character. Then God is seen primarily as the one who controls everything for the purpose of bringing glory to God's self. God becomes a tyrant who demands that humans act self-sacrificially to obey arbitrary laws. If God is *love*, then what God commands are expressions of God's commitment to human well-being.

From the Bible and Wesleyan theology, we see that God is love, and God's love is passionate concern for the comprehensive well-being of human beings—for each of us. There are four perspectives, or emphases, from which we can view God's love as passionate concern:

- *God's love is relational.* God has a passionate desire to draw us into a relationship with God's very self and to remove all obstacles between us. It is through this relationship that we can achieve the personal fulfillment God intends for us.
- *God's love is expressed in mercy, justice, and truth. Justice* is God's commitment to treating us according to who we

> **"Love is the very image of God;**
> **it is the brightness of his glory."**
> **–John Wesley**

are and what we do. *Mercy* is God's compassion for us as suffering and sinful human beings; it goes beyond *justice* in seeking to heal and transform us despite our rejection of God. *Truth* is God's reliability in being and action, so that we can always depend on God to act according to the divine character and purpose revealed through the Bible.

- *God's love is most profoundly revealed on the cross.* This is the deep, costly, self-sacrificial dedication to humanity that enters into the pain and suffering of the world in order to bring healing, reconciliation, and transformation.
- *God's love is not opposed to God's anger, because God's anger protects.* God's anger is directed at all that would destroy whatever prevents us from achieving the well-being that God intends for us.

These four perspectives are important in a society where the idea of divine love is often transformed into a vague concept of being nice, which turns God into an indulgent Father Christmas figure: unconcerned about sin and evil, his name can be invoked to support our own self-interest, and his primary role is our superficial happiness. The love of God revealed through the Bible is the very opposite of this, and it is only when this is understood that we can affirm with John Wesley that "love is the very image of God; it is the brightness of his glory."[4]

Loving God and Others

If God is love and we are created in the image of God, then God intends us to be full of love. As reflections of God's nature and character in this world, we are to demonstrate love for God and love for others. Love should motivate and shape all of our attitudes, thoughts, words, and actions. Yet in our culture today, love has been devalued. Popular music and films portray love largely in terms of romantic feelings and sexual desires. *I love you* often means "I love your body" or "I want to make love to you," and does not express a self-sacrificial commitment to the well-being of another. Even when love is directed beyond the narrow circle of family and friends, it is perceived to be acts of kindness or charity that do not have a substantial impact on one's own life. In other contexts, including Christian contexts, love is reduced to being nice, not rocking the boat, and pretending that problems do not exist. Such "love" ignores the reality of sin, evil, and suffering, and, as such, is not genuinely concerned about others' well-being. It often serves as a mask for deep, unresolved conflicts.

We need to reclaim a biblical and Wesleyan understanding of love. We will explore that in depth in the next chapter, but for now let's highlight some of the key features of biblical love:

- Love for God is centering one's life on God—giving God ultimate loyalty, living one's life to God's glory, and rejecting all competing loyalties.
- Love for God does not arise out of a sense of obligation; it arises out of gratitude for all that God has done in Christ, and it involves the whole of our being.

- Love for God is embodied in a life of prayer and thanksgiving, participation in communal worship, obedience to God's commandments, and trust in God's care.
- Love for others is the self-sacrificial commitment to the concrete and holistic well-being of all human beings, which includes spiritual, psychological, physical, and social dimensions.
- Love for others is not mere outward actions; it involves inner attitudes and motivations such as patience, humility, meekness, justice, self-sacrifice, and benevolence.
- Love for God gives rise to a concern for the earth and a care for its creatures, for these were created by God and are the subject of God's concern and care.

In summary, to say that we are created in the image of God is to say that we are created to reflect God's character by loving God and neighbor; to be a steward of all that God has entrusted to us, using it to promote the comprehensive well-being of others; and consequently, to be a source of blessing to the world. God's plan and desire are that we should live in union with God, in community with others, and in interdependence with the flourishing creation.

We were created for love, but there's a problem. Instead of loving God and others, we turn in upon ourselves. Instead of having God as the center of our lives and, as a result, directing our lives toward those God created and loves, we make self the center of our lives. This loving of self in the place of God, which also separates us from loving others, is the root of the sin that permeates our lives, communities, and societies. We see this in all spheres of human life. People who place their own financial gain at the center of their lives often neglect their spouses and children. The partners who place their pleasure at the center of their lives exploit the vulnerabilities of their dependent partners. As we move into the economic and social spheres, we see how corporations place profits before people, exploiting workers and customers. Politicians who are enamored with their own power and position promote laws that ensure they are reelected, even if these cause suffering to others. In worst-case scenarios, they deliberately scapegoat particular groups within society.

But there is good news. As we see in Wesley's writings, the core of the gospel message is that, despite our self-centeredness and its tragic consequences, God refuses to stop loving us; out of love, God acts to transform us so that God's love can become the center of our lives.

> ***God has a mission in the world,***
> ***and love is at the heart of that mission.***

God's Mission in the World

God has a mission in the world, and love is at the heart of that mission. Because of God's love for us, God desires to see our hearts transformed in holiness and new birth. This transformation of the human heart lies at the center of Wesley's thinking about God and humankind. If we are to understand what Wesley meant by this and—important for our study—how this relates to his understanding of the church, we need to explore Wesley's broader vision of what God is doing in the world, and how that is oriented toward the end of love.

Restoring Our Ability to Love

God's mission begins with grace. Our ability to love fully and completely is restored through God's grace. In other words, God refuses to reject human beings; God absorbs their rejection and continues to work in their lives, drawing them toward the original intention—that their lives be permeated by love. This begins with what Wesley refers to as *prevenient* or *preventing* grace. Both terms mean the grace that comes before or precedes. (*Prevenient* comes from Latin. In the eighteenth century, *prevent* also had the meaning of precede.) To understand what Wesley meant by this, we need to understand what Wesley meant by *grace*. Grace is the forgiving and transforming presence of the Spirit of God that draws us away from our self-centeredness into a dynamic relationship with God so that we become creatures saturated by God's love. Prevenient grace is God's presence and activity in all human beings that begins this process of leading us into a transforming relationship with God. Thus, for Wesley, wherever one sees people turning from self-centeredness toward a life of seeking the good of others, the Spirit of God is at work, regardless of whether that person is aware of God's grace, is a Christian, or has any knowledge of God. We can summarize this as follows:

- Grace is the presence and power of the Holy Spirit.
- Grace enlightens, enables, and transforms us.
- Grace enables us to become what God intended for us—creatures saturated with love.
- Grace is personal and therefore always dynamic and interactive.
- Grace is empowering but not compulsory.
- Grace is free, and its consequences are unpredictable.

- Grace is at work in the depth of the human person.
- Grace is at work in the interaction of people, communities, and societies.
- Grace is encountered through means, or instruments.

Grace is at work in the atheist doctor who, at risk of her own life, joins Doctors Without Borders to help sick and suffering people. It is in the Hindu politician who devotes his political career to uplifting the poor. Prevenient grace is also at work in and through the ministry of the church. It is at work, for example, in the lives of children growing up in the church who cannot recall when they came to personal faith in Christ; he seems to them to have been part of their lives since before they can remember. Perhaps more dramatically, it accompanies the preaching of the gospel so that it strikes deeply into people's lives, dramatically leading them to faith in Christ and transforming them. Grace transforms the self-centered businessperson intent on making a personal fortune into a person devoted to God and the well-being of others. Grace is as multifaceted as human beings are, encountering us at the point of our need and drawing us toward the God of love. Wesley called prevenient grace, or the grace that goes before, the presence and activity of the Holy Spirit in all people, in all societies and all cultures, which precedes any human response or even understanding. It's the grace that sets us free and empowers us to respond to God's love. It's the activity of the Spirit seeking to draw people away from self-centeredness into a transforming relationship with God, which will liberate and empower them to love God and their fellows. Wesley's teaching about prevenient grace has many dimensions. The following are significant for our purposes:

- It creates in all human beings a sense of right and wrong.
- It brings a basic awareness of God's requirement that we love others as ourselves.
- It empowers all people to put this basic requirement into practice.
- It creates a desire for a relationship with God, even when people are unable to express this desire.
- It prepares the way for the coming of a fuller revelation of God's intention for humanity.

We find in all people and in all societies a strange and unstable mix of the effects of human self-centeredness and the grace that goes before. It should not surprise us to find people who have no contact with Christianity, of another faith or no faith, who live out the Golden Rule. In a number of his writings, Wesley contrasts positively the levels of justice, mercy, and truth found in non-Christian societies with the injustice, cruelty, and deception found in the "Christian" societies of Europe. All societies evidence the unloving, selfish nature of humankind, but also the presence of prevenient grace whereby the ability to love God and others has begun to be restored.

God, Israel, and Love in the Bible

Although God relates to all human beings in the grace that goes before, God chose to relate in a particular way to the people of Israel by entrusting them with a covenant relationship and instructions for living in love of God and love of neighbor. God's relationship with Israel is perhaps best understood as a more focused expression of prevenient grace, preparing the way for the coming of Christ. In Wesley's understanding, God prepared for the coming of Christ by revealing to Israel a more detailed account of how God intends human beings to live. The Ten Commandments and ethical laws found in Exodus through Deuteronomy, as well as in the writings of the prophets, teach what it means to love God and our fellow human beings. They are an explanation of what love requires in specific circumstances. For example, if one loves one's neighbors one will refrain from stealing from them. The moral laws then go into more detail, with, for example, commands to care for the poor, widows, orphans, and migrants.

Many Christians today find the laws for Israel in the Old Testament difficult to understand, and at least some of them seem outdated. Wesley approached the Old Testament laws by interpreting them in light of three categories: the *moral law*, the *ceremonial/ritual law*, and the *civil/political law*. The ceremonial law refers to the various religious rituals, ceremonies, and related regulations. The civil laws are those laws that relate to the ordering of the civil society in Israel's time period. And the moral law was timeless and universal, applying to all of humankind. Wesley's identification of the moral law showed how God's intention was to enable Israel and all of humanity to become creatures of love.

The division of the Old Testament laws into three categories is not original to Wesley; it can be found in the Articles of Religion of the Church of England and goes back at least to Thomas Aquinas in the thirteenth century. This approach to the Old Testament argues that, while the ceremonial and civil laws were applicable only to Israel, the moral laws have abiding significance as they reflect the moral character of God who is love. As Wesley realized, it is not always easy to decide which category a particular law belongs to; in fact, some laws contain moral, ceremonial, and civil aspects. An interesting example of this is the law of the Sabbatical and

Jubilee years (Exod 23:10-11; Lev 25:1-55; Deut 15:1-18). Like the Sabbath day, aspects of these laws can be seen to be ceremonial, part of Israel's ritual life. They also had specific civil dimensions, making provisions for release from debt, emancipation of slaves, and return of land to its original owners. Yet the core of these provisions was an expression of love to the poor and needy, those who had suffered hard times, and to the land itself. Wesley often summed up the requirements of the moral law in three concepts: *justice*, *mercy*, and *truth*. There are examples of all of these in the Old Testament laws. *Justice* required that people accused of crimes receive a fair trial. It also required that special attention be given to the vulnerable members of society to ensure that they were not exploited. *Mercy* went beyond this and sought to provide for the needs of those who were excluded from wealth and power. Farmers were instructed to leave part of the produce in the fields for the poor, the widows, the orphans, and the migrants. The same groups were named, alongside the Levites, as beneficiaries of Israel's tithes. *Truth* required honesty in all areas of life; thus the Israelites were forbidden to use false measures or weights.

In Wesley's understanding, God's intent was that Israel should be a preliminary embodiment of the divine love that pointed beyond itself to the coming of the Messiah. The repeated failure of the people of Israel to live in conformity to the entirety of the law gave rise to longing for a new era in which God would transform the human heart. This dynamic is portrayed in the writings of the prophets. Jeremiah is a helpful example. Jeremiah 2 describes God's love for the people of Israel and their constant rejection of God— the source of their life—in favor of other gods. This turning away from God manifested in the adoption of a self-centered lifestyle built on exploitation of the poor and vulnerable (Jer 5:26-28;

9:1-6; 22:11-17). Jeremiah, reluctantly and with deep empathy for his people, announces God's judgment. However, judgment is not the final word, and he speaks of the restoration of the people and the renewal of the covenant. This hope for the future reaches its culmination in the prophecy of a new covenant:

> No, this is the covenant that I will make with the people of Israel after that time, declares the LORD. I will put my Instructions within them and engrave them on their hearts. I will be their God, and they will be my people. They will no longer need to teach each other to say, "Know the LORD!" because they will all know me, from the least of them to the greatest, declares the LORD; for I will forgive their wrongdoing and never again remember their sins.
>
> (Jer 31:33-34)

In Wesley's understanding, this hope, expressed in a variety of forms, pointed toward something dramatically new in God's loving interaction with humanity.

The Kingdom of Grace and Love

The dramatically new thing happened with the coming of Jesus. It was the inauguration of the kingdom of God's grace and love. God was doing a new thing, but it was the same God who had been in covenant with Israel that was doing this new thing. There is both continuity and discontinuity between God's relationship with Israel and the new thing done in Jesus. The hopes of the Old Testament are taken up and transformed; this is an expression of God's continuing faithfulness to the people of Israel. However, as in the Old Testament, love remains central to the life, ministry, and message of Jesus. Out of deep love and compassion for the needy, he heals the sick, feeds the hungry, opens the eyes of the blind, and

> *Jesus Christ is the incarnation of divine love. His life, as it climaxes with the crucifixion, embodies what it means to love God and one's neighbor.*

raises the dead. He lived in solidarity with the outcasts of society. He instructed his followers to live a life of love, not only for their neighbors but also for their enemies. He came to serve and give his life for others and called his followers to do the same by taking up their crosses and following him in the self-sacrificial commitment to the well-being of their fellows.

The dramatic newness of what happened in Jesus can be seen from a number of perspectives:

- Jesus Christ is the incarnation of divine love. His life, as it climaxes with the crucifixion, embodies what it means to love God and one's neighbor.
- Jesus Christ comes as the great prophet who reveals the depth of the moral law by emphasizing the significance of the internal motives that underlie external obedience.
- Jesus Christ comes as the great priest whose death brings forgiveness of sin.
- Jesus Christ comes as the king who reigns within us to transform us so that we obey the moral law.
- Jesus Christ rises from the dead, victorious over sin and evil.

- The Spirit comes at Pentecost to transform us from the inside out so that we can overcome the power of sin in our lives.

The kingdom of God's grace is a continuation and expansion of the reality inaugurated with God's revelation to Israel, culminating in the death and resurrection of Jesus Christ. But this kingdom also manifests in human hearts, as individuals become creatures who love. The kingdom of God's grace enters into the human person to bring about fundamental transformation of inner motives, desires, attitudes, and attraction, which leads to a radical change in behavior. Behavior will no longer be characterized by selfish, inward focus, but by love for God and love for neighbor. This change in people's behavior will lead to the transformation of societies and cultures, as those who have been transformed by God promote justice, mercy, and truth in all dimensions of society. Thus for Wesley, Christ came to destroy sin and evil by spreading "the fire of heavenly love over all the earth."[5] To return to our earlier discussion, the coming of the kingdom of God's grace within people liberates them from the power of sin and evil, enables and empowers them to love God and their fellows, and renews them so that they become a source of blessing to the world. In short, they transform so that they reflect God's character and represent God's interests as they participate in what God is doing in the world.

Wesley was convinced that the change within people brought about by Christ would lead to God's will being done on earth as it is in heaven and that "love is the essence of heaven."[6] He hoped for a time when love would permeate human societies so that they would become characterized by justice, mercy, and truth. Wesley described this vision of a transformed world, drawing on a variety of biblical passages, in his sermon "Scriptural Christianity": he looked forward to a time of peace when war, violence, injustice, and oppression are no more; when compassion and mercy replace cruelty; and when all speech is peaceful, kind, and honest. Here are Wesley's words:

> Assume that the fullness of time has now arrived and that the prophecies have been fulfilled. What a great prospect is this coming reality! The effect of righteousness will be peace, and "the result of righteousness, quietness and trust forever." There will be no more clamor of weapons, no "garments soaked in blood." "The very memories of enemies will have perished." Wars will cease from the earth. Neither are there any internal feuds, no brother attacking brother, no nation or city divided against itself and destroying itself. Civil discord will have come to an end forever, and there will be no one left either to destroy or harm others. In that day, there is no cruelty to "make the wise foolish," no illegal seizures to "grind the face of the poor." There will be no robbery or wrongdoing; no plundering or injustice, all people will be content with what they have. In that time "righteousness and peace will kiss each other." These blessings will "take deep root and fill the land; righteousness spring out of the earth and peace will look down from heaven."
>
> And with righteousness and justice, there will also be mercy. The earth will no longer be full of violent haunts.... Even if there were any provocation, there will be nobody who pays back evil for evil, not a single person— for all will be as innocent as doves. Being filled with peace and joy in believing, and united in one body, by one Spirit, they will all love each other as sisters and brothers. They will all be of one heart and soul. "Everything they own will be held in common." There will be no one among the redeemed company that will have any need, for all will love their

neighbors as themselves. Furthermore, all people will walk by one rule—"In everything, do unto others as you would have them do to you."

Consequently no unkind word can ever be heard among the redeemed—no accusing tongues, controversy, abusive language, or slander. Rather all will "open their mouths with wisdom, and the teaching of kindness will be on their tongues." The redeemed are equally incapable of deception or dishonest cunning guile. Their love is genuine. Always their words will truthfully express their thoughts, opening a window into their inner self, so that whosoever wishes may look into their hearts and see that only love and God are there.[7]

This vision was no more realistic in Wesley's time than it is today. Britain was involved in numerous wars; there was political instability and even rebellion; corruption and crime were rife; the wealth gap between rich and poor was vast; the poor were exploited and oppressed; inhumanity and cruelty pervaded much of society. Yet Wesley was convinced this could be changed. He had experienced God's transforming work in his own life and had seen how God transformed the lives of others. With God this was possible. Our contemporary world faces conflicts and tensions at all levels. Wars and violence continue to claim the lives of thousands. Oppression and injustice are features of many societies. Racism infects many societies. People, particularly women and children, are trafficked for exploitation in the sex industry. The gap between rich and poor continues to grow. The vulnerable are exploited. Religious minorities suffer discrimination and persecution. In many parts of the world, the LGBTQ community faces personal and, in some cases, institutional violence. Crime, violence, and terror—both internationally and locally—are part of the everyday lives of many people.

As Wesley viewed the influence of a revival of Christianity, of which Methodism was a part, he became convinced that he was living at the beginning of a process of worldwide transformation. From the perspective of some two hundred fifty years later, we can see that Methodism and its associated movements had—and continue to have—significant impact on human societies. To name just a few examples: European Methodists have been actively engaged in providing hospitality to migrants fleeing war, violence, and poverty. The United Methodist Church has been promoting reconciliation between Russians and Ukrainians after the conflicts in and annexation of Crimea by Russia. In the Democratic Republic of the Congo, ministries of The United Methodist Church provide for care and healing of victims of civil conflicts, not least the many women who were systematically raped. People are working against human trafficking and caring for its victims in the sex industry. There are numerous programs to care for the poor and the hungry. Numerous educational projects provide for the development of future leaders. Methodists have been involved in struggling for justice in diverse contexts, including apartheid in South Africa and the civil rights movements in the US.

While Methodists have not had the pervasive transforming effect Wesley hoped for, they have made an impact when they have become like "boiling water...penetrated and heated by the fire of love."[8]

Wesley's hope for the transformation of people, leading to the transformation of societies and cultures, was not his ultimate hope. For him, this was just the foretaste of a far greater transformation: the coming of the kingdom of glory when Christ returns. Wesley's views of the return of Christ and associated events are rather complex, speculative, and at times not very clear. He seems to have changed his mind over the years. Perhaps the most significant change in his thought was a move from seeing the final destiny of transformed humanity as being in heaven in the presence of God to seeing their final destiny as part of a transformed new creation permeated by the presence of God. The complex and speculative details are not as important as the vision of a new heaven and a new earth. This vision has four key aspects:

First, it is preceded by judgment. Judgment is not a popular theme in much contemporary Christianity. It is often regarded as old-fashioned and extremist. However we picture judgment, it is an important part of Wesley's theology for two reasons: (1) judgment means we are responsible before God for how we have lived; (2) judgment is the final removal of sin and evil from this world.

Second, the new creation is not limited to humanity. Wesley's vision included the resurrection of animals and the transformation of all creatures. He recognized that this was a mystery beyond our understanding.

Third, in the new creation there is no more sin, suffering, and evil. It is the triumph of God's love over all that opposes it.

Fourth, the ultimate goal is "a deep, an intimate, an uninterrupted union with God; a constant communion with the Father and his Son Jesus Christ, through the Spirit; a continual enjoyment of the Three-One God, and of all the creatures in him!"[9]

God's ultimate purpose is the transformation of all things as they are permeated by the presence of God who is love.

Conclusion

Let us briefly review what we have discovered through this chapter.

First, the character of God is best described by the radical love revealed on the cross, and thus, love is the foundation and goal of all of God's intentions and activity in this world.

Second, God's intention in creation is that human beings should reflect God's character of love and represent God's interests by embodying love for God and their fellow human beings. In doing this, they are a source of blessing to the world.

Third, human beings have failed to do this and, instead, are characterized by deep self-centeredness; but God refuses to give up on humanity and acts in grace to liberate human beings from our self-centeredness.

Fourth, the transformation of individuals through God's love has as its consequence the transformation of societies and cultures so that they express love through justice, mercy, and truth.

In the next chapter, we will explore in more detail how we as persons find our place in what God is doing in the world. These two chapters are the basis for the rest of the book, which will explore how the church in its different forms participates in what God is doing.

2

A LIFE SATURATED WITH THE LOVE OF GOD

Imagine that you are riding an elevator to the lobby of a building. On the tenth floor, the doors open and another person gets into the elevator with you. As the door closes, the person asks you, "Could you please answer a question for me? What is a Christian?" Knowing you have only the time it takes to get from the tenth floor to the lobby, how would you answer such a question?

When John Wesley described what it means to be a Christian, he often employed two basic descriptions, though his exact wording varied. The first description is one who loves God and, as a result, loves his neighbors as himself. In *A Plain Account of Christian Perfection*, Wesley writes,

> A Methodist is one who loves the Lord his God with all his heart, with all his soul, with all his mind, and with all his strength. God is the joy of his heart, and the desire of his soul. . . .

And loving God, he "loves his neighbour as himself"; he loves every man as his own soul. He loves his enemies, yea, and the enemies of God. And if it be not in his power to "do good to them that hate" him, yet he ceases not to "pray for them," though they spurn his love, and still "despitefully use him, and persecute him."[1]

The second description is one who has the mind of Christ and seeks to do the will of God. Wesley also states,

Agreeable to this his one desire is the one design of his life; namely, "to do, not his own will, but the will of Him that sent him." His one intention at all times and in all places is, not to please himself, but Him whom his soul loveth."[2]

In a number of his writings, Wesley explores these descriptions in more detail. It is significant that his focus is not on particular beliefs and religious practices but on the transformation of a person's character. Recalling what we discussed in the first chapter, we could say that, from a Wesleyan perspective, a Christian is one who has been caught up into God's purpose of transforming human beings and societies so that their lives are saturated by the love of God that was revealed in the life, death, and resurrection of Jesus.

In this chapter, we will look at two themes. The first is what it means to love God and neighbor. The second is how God transforms us so that we become permeated, or saturated, by love.

A Life Shaped by Love

When Wesley described a Christian as someone who loves God and their neighbors, he was not merely referring to outward

> ## *A Christian is one whose character is shaped by love from the inside out.*

behavior. He meant that love is the central motivating and directing influence in the life of a Christian. A Christian is one whose character is shaped by love from the inside out. Love then shapes our attitudes, our desires, our emotional responses, our expectations, and our hopes. A character permeated by love manifests in a lifestyle of loving activity. Or, to use another favorite expression of Wesley, a Christian is one who has the "mind of Christ" (that is, a mind permeated by love) and walks as Jesus did. The outer and the inner dimensions are inseparably connected, so that a transformed mind will express itself in transformed actions and a transformed way of life. It is never enough to do good as a means to be well thought of and to gain favor. Kind and helpful acts may never create in us a heart full of love, but a heart filled with love will always move a Christian to kind and helpful action.

A life permeated by love has its roots in a relationship with God who is love. From a deep recognition of and response to God's love for us, we are motivated and empowered to love God and all who are loved by God. It thus arises out of an awareness of the amazing reality that the Creator of the universe passionately desires to have a deeply personal relationship with us, despite our failures, rejection, rebellion, and brokenness. God, in Christ, took upon God's very self the pain and suffering of our self-centeredness, with its rejection of God, and the abuse and misuse of our fellow human beings; not only our failings but those of all humanity. The Spirit of God is at work within us, alluring and drawing us into an ever deeper relationship with God that liberates us from our self-centeredness, heals our brokenness, and empowers us to love God in response.

Loving God

God's love for us motivates and liberates us to love God in return. To love God is to place God and God's concerns at the center of our lives, thus reshaping our lives. This relationship of love is multidimensional and includes the following:

- *Gratitude* for God's love for us;
- Living in constant *fellowship* with God through regular prayer, meditation, and worship;
- Growing in *knowledge* of God;
- *Trust* in God's presence, care, and concern for us even in difficult and complex circumstances;
- *Sharing* our difficulties, struggles, anger, and complaints with God;
- Giving God the primary *loyalty* in all areas of our lives.
- *Seeking* to know and do God's will;
- *Obeying* God's commandments;
- Living all of our lives to the *glory* of God;
- *Costly self-denial* in relation to all that contradicts our relationship with God.

The fruit of such a relationship with God is, Wesley argued, true happiness. As we grow in our loving relationship with God, we will be transformed so that we begin to share and imitate God's loving character; we are changed into the image of God who is love. God's love begins to permeate our lives, expressing itself in and through us so that we increasingly share God's love for all humanity and all of God's creation.

Loving All Human Beings

As we grow in our relationship with God and become saturated by divine love, we participate in God's love for human beings. Crucially, this raises the question of what Wesley meant by love for human beings. *Love* is a deep commitment to the well-being of others. Wesley preached, "Whosoever feels the love of God and man shed abroad in his heart, feels an ardent and uninterrupted thirst after the happiness of all his fellow-creatures. His soul melts away with the very fervent desire which he hath continually to promote it; and out of the abundance of the heart his mouth speaketh."[3]

Wesley's understanding of love of neighbor can be seen in four dimensions: a commitment to the well-being of others; care for all people; the involvement of our whole life and self; and self-sacrifice.

The first dimension is a comprehensive *commitment to the well-being of others*. Wesley referred to doing good to people's bodies and souls. In contemporary terminology, we could speak of the psychological, physical, social, and spiritual dimensions of a person's life. In his day, Wesley was enamored of health and the latest medical advances. One of his early publications was *Primitive Physic: Or An Easy and Natural Method of Curing Most Diseases*. Wesley was interested in the well-being of body and mind, as well as spirit.

The second dimension extends the commitment to well-being to be inclusive and universal of *all* people. Wesley went out of his way to stress that *neighbor* did not merely refer to people one knew and liked but to all people everywhere. This included people of different nations, religions, classes, and lifestyles. Love is to be directed to not only friends but also strangers and enemies; not only those with whom we agree but also those with whom we disagree, no matter how strongly. It is directed not only to the good but also to the evil—even those we consider to be God's enemies. Our love is to be directed to every human being that God has made. This does not mean that we do not have a particular love for, and loyalty to, members of our families, our fellow Christians, fellow citizens, and our friends; but this particular love ought not to preclude our commitment to all people.

Third, love of neighbor is to pervade all dimensions of our lives. True love demands the totality of all we think, say, and do. It should shape our personal and family lives, our professional lives, our politics, and our leisure. We may not compartmentalize the love of God, segregating it from other aspects of our character. As God is love, we become manifestations of this total and all-consuming love.

Fourth, love of neighbor is "disinterested," and, hence, it may be costly. Wesley stated in his sermon "On Love,"

> Therefore, if you love God with all your heart, you cannot so wrong him as to rob him of his glory, by taking to yourself what is due to him only. You will own that all you are, and all you have, is his; that without him you can do nothing; that he is your light and your life, your strength and your all; and that you are nothing, yea, less than nothing, before him. And if you love your neighbour as yourself, you will not be able to prefer yourself before him.[4]

Wesley also meant that in doing good for others, we should not act for our own benefit in any way. This includes acting because of the sense of satisfaction and fulfillment experienced when one has done something good. While these feelings may be the fruit of our actions, they ought not to be the motive. Because it is aimed exclusively at the good of the other, loving action can, and often does, entail self-sacrifice.

Attitudes, Words, and Actions

When love of all people directs and suffuses our lives, it shapes our attitudes, our words, and our actions. God's transforming love reorients our lives, stimulating the development and growth of attributes that express this love. Wesley named numerous characteristics in a wide variety of his sermons, including gentleness, meekness, humility, long-suffering, patience, deadness to the world, tenderness, sympathy, compassion, condescension (not thinking of oneself more highly than others), hope, kindness, fidelity, goodness, temperance, thinking the best of others, trust, and self-control. He also regularly summarized the character of a life transformed by divine love by referring to three overarching characteristics that can be related to attitudes, actions, and words: justice, mercy, and truth.

Wesley was deeply aware of the power and importance of our words, whether spoken or written. Our words can be used to build up and to heal; but they can also be used to degrade and destroy. Genuine love will be expressed in our words, particularly as they relate to those with whom we disagree. Wesley's reflections on how we use words have even greater significance in our age of social media. Words written in blogs, posts, and tweets rapidly spread beyond the control of the author and can affect people across the globe. The insignificance of the context of the person addressed and the public nature of social media intensify the potential harm done by careless words. People will post or tweet a comment that they would seldom, or never, utter in the presence of the persons concerned.

> **A person permeated by love will refuse to speak or write unkindly, negatively, or destructively about another.**

A person permeated by love will refuse to speak or write unkindly, negatively, or destructively about another. This is particularly so in the context of disagreements over issues of religion and theology. In such cases, people will address the issues concerned and not attack a person who disagrees with them. Positive and gracious words, directed by love, will, whether in the presence or the absence of the persons involved, conform to the triad of justice, mercy, and truth.

Truth is the first criterion of loving words. All our words should be truthful. All forms of deception and dishonesty are to be avoided. This includes the use of partial truths; selective quotations that distort the intention of the originator; the twisting of the truth to serve particular personal, political, or even religious goals; and all attempts to create a false or partial impression of a person, an event, or any phenomenon. If our words are to be truthful in an age of information overload and "fake news," we need to pay careful attention to discerning what is true and what is false in what we hear, read, and see. An important aspect of this is a self-critical listening to those who hold different and even contradictory views to our own. We not only need to be sure that our words are truthful, we also have an obligation to promote the truth. One way we do this is to warn others of error and sin. Wesley wrote an entire sermon dedicated to the topic of "The Duty of Reproving our Neighbour." In our contemporary age, where tolerance has become a predominant virtue, some of what Wesley proposes seems to be an offensive intrusion into a person's private life. However, genuine love—particularly in the context of the church—requires us to address behavior patterns or actions that are harmful to others or self-destructive. This is true, not only in a personal context, but also in social, cultural, and political spheres. As Wesley emphasized, such speaking the truth must be done in love and humility, recognizing one's own weaknesses and failures. This is also a practice in the community of faith, and not simply a matter of one person judging the behaviors of others.

The second criterion of loving words is *justice*. In Wesley's teaching, justice refers to giving people their due. The Golden Rule is the essence of justice; so the way we use words means that we will speak of others as we wish people would speak of us. *Justice* needs to be added to *truth*, for truthful words can be used in an unjust manner. People's arguments must be carefully evaluated in their original context. In discussion and debate, we must focus on arguments and not assault. It is fundamentally unjust to engage in personal attacks, to denigrate others, or to misrepresent their intentions. Spreading rumors or telling negative stories about people, even if they are true, is contrary to justice, for people can be hurt and their reputations damaged without them having the ability to respond or defend themselves. Criticism and complaints need to be dealt with in person. The criterion of *justice*, like that of *truth*, calls us to use our words to promote justice in the communities and societies in which we live.

Truth and *justice* on their own are inadequate criteria, for Wesley was aware that truthful and even just words can be used destructively; hence the final criterion is *mercy* or *compassion*. The criterion of *compassion* can be used in three ways: (1) the way we describe people, events, or situations. Compassion dictates that we respect and regard the people we find in a wide variety of challenging situations. (2) The way we interpret the words and actions of others; compassion requires that we understand the contexts in which people are found. Understanding where people come from is essential to understanding who they are. It means not making assumptions about people, not ascribing negative characteristics, and giving people the benefit of the doubt. Essentially, compassion and mercy are nonjudgmental and unconditional. Finally, (3) compassion requires that our words be used to relieve the needs and sufferings of others. Take note, however, compassion and mercy are not about doing nice things for people in need; it means that we enter into relationship with people and work together to find lasting solutions and radical improvement.

Wesley had little time for small talk and argued that all our conversations should have a positive intention, either for ourselves (increasing our knowledge or improving our character) or for the good of others. While we may not follow his instruction to reject all small talk, we should always bear in mind the impact of our words on others and seek to use our words in the service of love.

When love permeates our entire being, it will prevent us from acting in ways that knowingly cause harm, injury, or grief to another person. When love informs all dimensions of our lives, then our work, politics, leisure, and faith will reflect this love; and we will not support policies, institutions, or practices that exploit, degrade, misuse, or unjustly treat anyone. In our complex global community, this kind of love is especially challenging, and also more important than ever. The powerful love that defines our discipleship has the power to transform our world.

Wesley described the positive requirement of love this way:

> It guides him to an uniform practice of justice and
> mercy.... It constrains him to do all the possible good, of
> every possible kind, to all men; and makes him invariably
> resolved in every circumstance of life to do that, and that
> only, to others which, supposing he were himself in the same
> situation he would desire they should do to him.[5]

This form of the Golden Rule included acts of charity (see Matt 25): feeding the hungry, caring for the stranger, providing for the poor, visiting the sick and lonely, and housing the homeless. But it went beyond that. Early Methodism supported numerous projects to enable and support the poor and marginalized. These included medical care, job-creation projects, schools, and a micro-lending system. It also led Wesley and early Methodists into political activism as they worked for the abolition of slavery.

Displays of God's love through our words and actions should not be visible simply in special projects and grandiose efforts but in every dimension of our lives. Kind words, compliments, loving gestures, and random acts of kindness can easily be shared with others many times each day. Love that permeates to our very soul will find expression in multiple ways.

One other significant sign of a truly loving nature, according to Wesley, was how Christians use their money. He famously argued that Christians should earn all they can, save all they can (not in the modern sense of investing money but in the eighteenth-century sense of living frugally), and give all they can. For Wesley, the way we use our money is a key indicator of whether we truly love God and our neighbors. A failure to give was a clear indication of a failure to love. Focusing only on earning all we can and saving all we can indicates that money has assumed the number one priority in our lives. It has become our god; love of money has driven out our love for God. Additionally, when we keep our financial resources and use them only for ourselves, we do not self-sacrificially love our neighbors.

Transformed by God's Love

In much the same way that it is impossible for us to achieve perfection in this lifetime by our own means and merit, Wesley's ideal of total and complete embodiment of God's love is impossible apart from God's love. Wesley discovered this himself. In 1725, Wesley was a twenty-two-year-old student resolved to be a real Christian, a person whose inner and outer life was shaped by love for God and neighbor. This set him on a long and, at times, difficult path, which culminated in his discovery in 1738 that the key to transformation was the personal experience of God's accepting and transforming love. Just as we are being perfected in God's love, so, too, we are being filled with grace in love.

In this section we will examine Wesley's understanding of the transforming power of God's love. First, we will focus on the way that God's love reaches and changes us. Second, we will look at the means we use to encounter and express God's love.

The Way of God's Love

Wesley's starting point is what has traditionally been described as "original sin." For Wesley, the doctrine of original sin was one of the essential doctrines of the Christian faith. In fact, the only major work of academic theology that Wesley wrote was on original sin. *Original sin* has been variously defined and described over the centuries. Many Christians today find it a depressing and even destructive doctrine that we should leave behind. Why was it so important for Wesley, and why is it important for us today? As I argued in the first chapter, to confess that we are sinners is to recognize that within the core of the human person there is a self-centering dynamic. Instead of being creatures who love God and our neighbors, we focus on ourselves, our interests, our needs, our desires, and our pleasures. The doctrine of original sin emphasizes three facets of this inward focus. The first facet reveals that self-centeredness is true of all human beings, in all societies and cultures. No human society is free from the impact of self-centeredness. The second facet is that it pervades all aspects of the human person. Self-centeredness shapes our thoughts, desires, wishes, words, and actions. The third facet is that we, individually, are powerless to do anything to change this situation. According to Wesley, we can set out on the way toward deep transformation only when we recognize the extent to which sin permeates and shapes our lives.

This may seem a bit extreme. After all, when we look at our lives, we see that we do not act only in self-centered ways. We are capable of love, self-sacrifice, justice, mercy, and truth. When we look at human history, we do not see only wars, injustice, oppression, and genocide; we also see movements for justice, peace, compassion, and integrity. We see this, not only in societies influenced by Christianity, but also in those that have had little or no contact with the gospel. Wesley would agree. In a number of his writings, he praised the justice, mercy, and truth that was to be found in non-Christian societies, in comparison to the injustice, cruelty, and corruption that characterized the so-called Christian societies of Europe. The doctrine of original sin does not mean that people and societies are uniformly evil; it means that, in their fallen condition, they are a mixture of good and evil. Good and evil, selflessness and selfishness, dynamically interact with each other. In some situations or aspects of society, good seems to dominate, while in others, evil does. As noted in the first chapter, this is an expression of the reality that God is at work in all people, drawing them into a transforming relationship with God. This is what Wesley described as prevenient or preventing grace. It is important to repeat that, for Wesley, this is God's presence in all people, which enables and motivates them to varying degrees to turn from their self-centeredness.

In a specific way, God's grace accompanies the proclamation of the gospel in whatever form is necessary or helpful. As people hear the message that God has acted in Jesus Christ to overcome sin and evil to usher in God's reign of love, people experience an intensification of the presence and work of the Spirit in their lives. As with all the work of God's Spirit, people can resist or open themselves to what God is doing. If they respond positively to the work of the Spirit, Wesley described them as being awakened people becoming aware of their need, of their sin, of God's love for them, and of God's desire to enter into a relationship with them.

The "good news" is that God so loves us that God has taken our sin upon God's very self. In Christ, God absolves our rejection of God and others and offers us forgiveness and the possibility of new life. In response to this message, grace enables us to begin to turn from our self-centeredness and to seek after God until we come to a place of faith. Faith is the deep inner conviction that God does love us, that God has forgiven us, and that God welcomes us as children of God. Wesley argued that as we come to God, so God gives us the assurance that we are the dearly loved children of God. While our awareness of this assurance may grow or weaken, and even at times disappear, God still loves us and desires a relationship with us. This process of being forgiven and accepted by God is what has historically been described as *justification*. God reestablishes us in right relationship.

> ## *Faith is the deep inner conviction that God does love us, that God has forgiven us, and that God welcomes us as children of God.*

The gospel message, the "good news," is that not only are we reestablished into a right relationship with God and our sin forgiven, but also that God is at work within us to transform us. God redirects our focus from the self to love God and our neighbors. God renews, empowers, and enables us to overcome sin and to be transformed into the image of God revealed in Jesus the Christ. This is what Wesley described as the new birth. Particularly early in his ministry, Wesley tended to argue that this is a clearly marked event, followed by a process of growth. He qualified this later in his life as he recognized that people could experience God's grace more gradually and could respond over a period of time. Yet he insisted that there must be a singular point of transformation for change. For many people, particularly people who grow up in the church, there is no clear dramatic event to which they can point. They can see God at work in their lives over time, and their response to God takes different forms. As they look back, they are assured that God has been at work, that they have been forgiven, that God has affirmed them as the children of God, that their lives have been reoriented toward God and others, and that now they experience God's transforming power in their lives.

The new birth, like a natural birth, is only the beginning. It leads us into a lifelong process of growth and development in our relationship with God so that divine love begins to permeate and reshape our lives. We can understand this from two perspectives. The first is that love for God and others increasingly overcomes our self-centeredness, transforming our attitudes, words, and actions. The second is that throughout our lives we will encounter new situations, issues, and problems. These are new opportunities to discover what it means to love God and our fellow human beings.

This process of change is what Wesley described theologically as *sanctification*. Wesley went a step further and argued that there is another development in a Christian's life, what he called *entire sanctification*, or *perfection in love*. This is transformation where love so dominates a person's life that it drives out all self-centeredness. He proposed that in most cases this occurs just before a person dies, but he argued that it can occur anytime during a person's life. This teaching proved controversial in Wesley's time and continues to be today, regarding exactly what Wesley meant and how this can be experienced in our lives. While there may not be a definitive answer, what is important is the conviction that the Holy Spirit can and does dramatically change people's lives as they seek a deeper and fuller relationship with God. We need to be open to such a change.

Change does not happen automatically. As we faithfully seek God, God's grace goes before us and comes to us. We do not earn this grace, but we come to a level of awareness that allows us to be open to it. Wesley promoted the practice of the means of grace—

corporate worship and prayer, participation in the Lord's Supper, fasting, Christian conference, joint acts of mercy—as a way of opening ourselves to this loving acceptance and transformation of God.

The Means of Growing in Love

Wesley understood Christianity to be active, not passive. Christians do not wait for God to act, but through faith, they act on behalf of God, empowered by God's Holy Spirit. Christianity is social, a shared experience. He claimed that there was no such thing as individual or personal holiness; we are a people of God. Only as we engage with other people and express our love of God through our love for our neighbors do we have the right to call ourselves Christian.

Wesley suggested that this active engagement takes structured forms: the *means of grace.* The means of grace are "outward symbols, words and actions that God has ordained to be the ordinary channels through which he might convey to us his prevenient, justifying, and sanctifying grace."[6] In order to understand what Wesley meant, we need to note the following features of the means of grace.

First, the means of grace are, at the same time, expressions of our love for God and our neighbors and the means through which we grow in our love for God and others.

Second, Wesley called for a balance in our lives between works of piety—the personal and inward ways we meet God, either individually or corporately—and works of mercy—personal and outward ways we express our faith in service to others, again alone or in relationship with others. Our faith-based activities shape us and prepare us to receive what God is working to do in us and with us. It is significant that Wesley prioritized acts of mercy over acts of piety. It is more important and of greater transforming significance to be actively involved in meeting the needs of others than it is to be involved in various religious activities.

This is especially important in our modern culture, where so much attention is given to beliefs and belonging over behavior. It is not enough to believe that Jesus Christ is the Son of God and to attend a worship experience when convenient; we must put our faith into action and serve others in the name of Christ. Wesley echoed James in a significant way: faith without works is dead (see Jas 2:17-26 NRSV).

Third, participation in the means of grace prepares us for the transforming work of God, remaking us in God's own image. The practice of the means of grace helps us discover the character of God and the discernment of God's will. Inward transformation results in outward expression. An analogy to this symbiotic relationship is breathing. With each inhalation, we are renewed and strengthened; with each exhalation we put faith into action and expend our energy, leading us to breathe in once again. No one may only inhale or only exhale. The rhythm and relationship of inhaling and exhaling is a wonderful illustration of the dynamic between works of piety and works of mercy.

Fourth, a Wesleyan understanding of the means of grace emphasizes both God's transforming work and our human activity. Through the means of grace, we do not earn God's favor, nor do we make ourselves more holy or acceptable. God's grace is indisputable; it is already offered to us. However, our ability to understand and accept God's grace can be severely limited. The practice of the means of grace through acts of piety and acts of mercy is essentially for our benefit. These acts make us ready to receive what God so deeply wishes to deliver. God enables us to respond and empowers us to love God and others through a variety of expressions.

Fifth, the goal of the means of grace is our transformation. God does not need or require our human expressions of faith and devotion. Our prayers, our worship, our service, our study, and our fellowship are not truly for God's benefit; they are for ours. God does not need transformation and change; we do. The means of grace are not a method of earning God's favor or showing off our religiosity or our generosity, but a pathway to open us (human beings) to all the blessings and perfecting love God freely gives.

Conclusion

The core of Wesley's understanding of Christianity is that God transforms human beings so that their lives become permeated by love for God and neighbor. This Wesleyan understanding has three key elements that we need to remember:

- *Transformation is interactive.* It starts with God's presence and action. We must respond to what God is doing; our positive response leads to an intensification of God's transforming presence.
- *Transformation involves a dynamic balance of inner and outer experience.* Inner change leads to change in our behaviors and practices; changes in our behaviors and practices reshape our character.
- *Transformation is pervasive.* God's transforming action is the fundamental redirection of our lives that permeates all dimensions of our existence.

3

WHERE IS THE CHURCH
IN ALL OF THIS?

What is the first thing that comes into your mind when you hear the word *church*?

- A local congregation of which you are a member?
- An imposing building near to where you live?
- A denomination—The United Methodist Church?
- All different denominations together as one community?
- The body made up of all true believers?
- Something quite different?

John Wesley declared in his sermon "Of the Church," "A more ambiguous word than this, the Church, is scarce to be found in the English language."[1] In this chapter, we will describe the core identity of the church from a Wesleyan perspective. As we proceed, we need to remember that what people think about the church is shaped more by concrete experiences than by theological reflection.

Wesley dealt with the ambiguity in our common use of the term *church* and examined how it is used in the New Testament. The core meaning for Wesley was "a congregation, or body of people, united together in the service of God."[2] He described how, in the New Testament, it can refer to a small group (even two or three people) gathered for worship, a larger community that meets regularly for worship, the Christians in a particular town or region—even if they do not all gather in the same location for worship together—or finally to "all the Christian congregations that are upon the face of the earth."[3] This is the "universal" church. In another sermon, "On Zeal," he stated that the church was established by God because "He saw it was 'not good for men to be alone,' . . . but that the whole body of his children should be 'knit together, and strengthened, by that which every joint supplieth.'"[4] They are "united by all kind of fellowship."[5] Wesley's focus was on a group of people from the general society, called out by the gospel to be with one another. This brought together into a new community people who, in the broader society, had great distance from one another. Even when separated by geographical distance, these people formed one community. This is especially important in our age of individualism and the focus on concepts of personal and private salvation. Solitary Christians are not "the church." Only together can we become the people God intends us to be.

Why is this important? Often we think of "churches"—in the plural—as different denominations and individual congregations. Wesley's starting point, in contrast, was that the purpose of the church is to bring people together to be with one another. All of our differences and our diversity are important and necessary for us to fulfill God's intention that we be together as the one body of Christ.

Who Are the People Brought Together?

In his sermon "Of the Church," Wesley expounded on some verses from Ephesians:

> I encourage you to live as people worthy of the call you received from God. Conduct yourselves with all humility, gentleness, and patience. Accept each other with love, and make an effort to preserve the unity of the Spirit with the peace that ties you together. You are one body and one spirit, just as God also called you in one hope. There is one Lord, one faith, one baptism, and one God and Father of all, who is over all, through all, and in all. (Eph 4:1-6)

The one body, Wesley argued, refers to the universal church made up of all Christians. The church is united by the presence and work of the one God who transforms all. These people share a common hope in the resurrection. They have one Lord. This does not mean merely that they acknowledge Christ in some sense; it means they live their lives in obedience to him. They have a common faith—not a set of theological views, but the shared personal trust in Christ for salvation. They share one baptism—for Wesley, the outward sign of God's grace given to the church. Finally, they have a common Father—not in a biological sense, but in the deep assurance that they are in every way the children of God. We can summarize this by saying that the church is made up of those who have been transformed by the Spirit of God through Christ; this common union with Christ brings them into relationship with one another. In our world today, Christians from Africa, Asia, South and Central America, Europe, and the United States can gather together to celebrate, worship, and give praise to God. Canadians and Mexicans and Russians and Chinese can set aside nationalities to embrace a deeper, greater spiritual unity in Christ. Those of different political parties, worldviews, cultures, life experiences, economic classes, and educational backgrounds can unite around a common faith in one God. Our differences pale in the light of our shared belief and baptism. Truly, by God's grace, we are made "one with Christ, / one with each other, / and one in ministry to all the world."[6]

> *The universal church of Jesus Christ is essentially bigger than any and all attempts on the part of human beings to comprehend it.*

In our daily lives, we do not encounter this universal church; we encounter the visible church. The visible church is a plethora of diverse communities and institutions that claim in various ways to be an expression of the invisible universal church, sometimes claiming to be *the* expression of the invisible universal church. The sheer diversity of beliefs and practices found in these churches raises the question of which of these communities might have a valid claim to be a genuine expression of the universal church. This question intensifies when we consider the obvious failures and limitations of these churches. Claims to be "the one true church" are fraught with peril. Churches have claimed to know the time for the end of the world, for the return of Christ, for right belief and behavior for all people, for the limits of blasphemy and sacrilege, and who belongs and who does not. No one denomination, congregation, or movement holds the authority to answer these questions. The universal church of Jesus Christ is essentially bigger than any and all attempts on the part of human beings to comprehend it.

When Wesley addressed this question, he often reflected on the description of the church taken from the Articles of Religion of the Church of England, which defines the visible church as "a congregation of faithful men."[7] For Wesley, the crucial phrase was "faithful men" (interestingly, in some references to this article he changed "men" to "people"). In his sermon "On the Church," he defined *faithful* as "men endued with living faith";[8] in other contexts, he referred to true believers. On one occasion, he referred to "true believers who have 'the mind that was in Christ' and 'walk as Christ walked.'"[9]

What is the significance of this? For Wesley it was twofold. First, the church is composed of all who have been genuinely transformed by the Spirit of God; so, therefore, institutional churches will welcome all such people into their communities. Second, only those who have been transformed by the grace of God are members of the community called "the church"; hence the institutional churches that are expressions of the universal church will give expression to the transforming work of the Spirit in their communal lives. These two affirmations shape a Wesleyan understanding of the church.

The Visible Face of the Church

What is the "public face" of the church? There are a variety of answers to this question, both negative and positive. There is no simplistic theological distinction between a genuine, *invisible* church of people transformed by the Spirit, and a *visible* church that is often compromised, broken, and sometimes completely wrong. Such simplistic description neither makes for good public relations nor provides a compelling witness of the church. What people see and experience is the basis of their evaluation of the church, and through it, their view and opinion of God.

The universal, visible church is revealed in the diversity of our institutional churches, denominations, and movements. Clearly, it is not perfect, and no segment holds a claim on the truth for all; but our strength is that the church universal is continuously in discussion and debate about truth, faithfulness, and witness. This results in the church universal seeking always and everywhere to understand and do the will of God.

Let us go back to the description of the church from the Anglican Articles of Religion. The full description is:

> The visible Church of Christ is a congregation of faithful men, in which the pure Word of God is preached, and the Sacraments be duly ministered according to Christ's ordinance, in all those things that of necessity are requisite to the same.
>
> As the Church of *Jerusalem, Alexandria,* and *Antioch,* have erred, so also the Church of *Rome* hath erred, not only in their living and manner of Ceremonies, but also in matters of Faith.[10]

Let us examine this statement in more detail. Congregations are visible representations of the universal church when they are made up of people of genuine faith, when the Word of God is preached in purity and when the sacraments are correctly administered.

The indication in the second paragraph is that people have not been faithful in their ceremonies, and that the sacraments have not been correctly administered. Additionally, "in matters of faith," the Word has not been purely preached. This indicated a common bias at the time the articles were written that only Protestant churches were true representatives of the invisible church. What is interesting for us is that Wesley left out the last paragraph when he prepared a revised version of the Articles of Religion for the Methodists in North America.[11] Wesley did allow that there were congregations in the Roman Catholic Church who were visible representatives of the true church. In fact, in a number of places he used Roman Catholics as outstanding examples of what it meant to be a faithful Christian.

Even more striking is that, while he kept the statement about the pure preaching of the word and the correct administration of the sacraments in his revised version of the articles, he stated that he would not "defend the accuracy of this statement."[12] Wesley had come to understand that faithful Christians might have very different understandings of what the "pure Word of God" taught and how the sacraments were to be celebrated. One example is in the institution of the Lord's Supper. Some churches felt strongly that Communion required a common loaf and a common cup—all participants eating from one loaf and drinking from one cup. *Intinction*, the dipping of bread in the cup, was a less popular, but common practice. Multiple loaves and multiple cups became accepted in larger congregations. The quality of wine, type of bread, and even questions of appropriate paten and chalice claimed great attention. Wesley viewed all these as distractions.

But more importantly, Wesley came to see the visibility of the church as something very different. Wesley focused his descriptions of the visible church on the phrase "faithful men," which he interpreted to mean people of genuine faith who live lives of holiness and love. Or, to use the terms we explored in the last chapter, they were people who had the mind of Christ and walked as he did. Participation in the means of grace through clear commitment to personal piety and acts of mercy defined this genuine faith. What people believed and professed resulted in clear and visible actions. The visibility of the church was not constituted of institutional structures or services of worship, but of the concrete lives of its members. In a poem entitled "Primitive Christianity" he put it this way:

> Ye different sects, who all declare,
> "Lo! Here is Christ!" or, "Christ is there!"
> Your stronger proofs divinely give,
> And show me where the Christians live.
>
> Your claim, alas! ye cannot prove,
> Ye want the genuine mark of love:
> Thou only, Lord, thine own canst show;
> For sure thou hast a Church below.[13]

In these words, Wesley reiterates his view that no one denomination or segment of the church holds the truth for all. The body of Christ cannot be divided. We may perceive different aspects of the divine, we may perform our rituals in different ways, we may hold particular beliefs to be sacred, and we may differ in our interpretations of Scripture, but none of this changes anything significant. Together, we are the children of God and the people of the Christian faith. Only God may determine what is true and beautiful and good and right. On earth, we join together in our churches to do our very best to make sense of God's will and God's work.

The distinguishing mark of the genuine, visible expression of the invisible church is love. In chapter 1, we saw how Wesley described

> **The distinguishing mark
> of the genuine, visible expression
> of the invisible church is love.**

a world permeated by love when God's reign has transformed all of life. The visible church is the community of people who are the foretaste of this transformation. It is the community that is visible by its concrete life of love, which is expressed inwardly among its members and outwardly toward those who are not (yet) members of the fellowship. An institutional church or denomination is a visible expression of the invisible universal church only to the extent that it:

- is characterized by ultimate loyalty to God revealed in the crucified and resurrected Christ, acknowledged in worship and devotion, and expressed in its life in the world;
- is characterized by a deep concern for, and the practical commitment to, the inclusive holistic well-being of its members;
- is engaged in an active, concrete, and holistic ministry of love with and to those outside the church.

This raises two key questions. First, how are we to understand the place of institutional structures at all levels, from congregations to denominations and beyond to interchurch and ecumenical groups? Second, how do we deal with the realities of the mixed character and failures of institutional churches at their various levels? We find answers to both these questions in John Wesley's writings.

The answer to the first question is that the various institutional structures, which are a mixture of elements ordained by God and created by human innovation, are there to foster our growth in love. They are the scaffolding that surrounds a new building as it is being constructed. The scaffolding is important because it facilitates the process of building, but what is really important is the construction that the scaffolding supports. At times then, scaffolding needs to be changed, added to, taken down, and put in new places for the process of building to continue. So it is with institutional church structures. They continue to have value and significance when they aid the community to embody love toward its members and the world outside. When they cease to have this function, it is time to change and redevelop them. In response to new situations and events, it might be necessary to develop quite new structures, and, therefore, different scaffolds.

Regarding the second question, Wesley acknowledged that the church was a mixed body, but he refused to allow this to become a means of justifying sin, corruption, and faithlessness within institutional churches and among church members. For Wesley, one of the greatest affronts to faithfulness by institutional churches were people who, Christians in name, demonstrated the opposite of divine love in lifestyle. For him, such people had left the church, even if they were still nominally members or even continued to be active in its structures.

Wesley's understanding can be seen in his interpretation of the parable of the wheat and the tares in Matt 13:24-30. This is one of the classic texts used throughout history to describe the church as a diverse body. In Matthew, Jesus compares the reign of God to a field in which a farmer sows wheat. While he is asleep, an enemy comes and sows tares or weeds in the field. These weeds look very much like wheat when they first sprout, so when the farm workers suggest that they should attempt to weed out the tares, the farmer replies that this cannot be done without damaging the wheat. Only when they are fully grown can they be distinguished easily; therefore, harvest is the time the two can be separated. In his *Explanatory Notes upon the New Testament*, Wesley goes beyond the text and adds thistles and brambles to the weeds and wheat. Unlike the tares, thistles and brambles can easily be distinguished from wheat. Wesley argues that the thistles and brambles are those whose lives are so far from the outward expression of divine love that they are clearly distinguished from true believers and, thus, can be separated from them. People represented by the tares are those who are not genuine believers but who outwardly conform to the gospel, or perhaps people seeking a transforming relationship with God who have not yet experienced it. Such people can remain in the church.

Wesley implemented a policy of discipline within early Methodism. Membership in Methodist societies was open to all who were seeking salvation, but they had to demonstrate the authenticity of their desire by doing no harm, doing all the good they could, and attending to the ordinances of God by participating in the life of the Methodist society and the church. Those who failed to do this, or those who no longer did so, lost their membership in the Methodist societies. It was quite common that when Wesley visited a Methodist society, he would examine the lives of the members, and those who did not live up to the lifestyle expected were excluded from the society until they reformed and began to give evidence of loving God and neighbor. It was expected of every Methodist that they would pray individually and with the community of faith, worship regularly and celebrate the Lord's Supper, fast twice weekly, study the Scriptures, serve the poor and destitute, be part of a class meeting for spiritual discernment and accountability, and tithe to the work of the church. This may sound rather harsh and strict to many contemporary Methodists, but it was simply basic in Wesley's day. In our own time, many claim that they do not have the time to devote much attention and engagement to such activities. Wesley would question the maturity of such Christians. While we will discuss this in more detail in a later chapter, the point for Wesley was that, if a person claimed to be a Methodist and a member of the visible church represented by the Methodist society, then he or she must visibly demonstrate this by a lifestyle permeated by love.

> *The church is called to be not only the embodiment of love but also the means that God uses to cultivate love.*

Cultivating Love:
The Church and the Means of Grace

Wesley's ideal for the church seems unreachable. In our local congregations and denominations, we don't have to look too deeply to discover much that is far from this ideal going on within the life of the church. From minor bickering through power struggles to various forms of abusive behavior, indications are that we have not achieved expansive love manifest in transformed lives. Sin clings to and distorts our best intended actions. Wesley was well aware of this. The church is called to be not only the embodiment of love but also the means that God uses to cultivate love. A key reason God brings people together in the church is that, through participation in community, they grow together in love.

Growth in holiness is not automatic, nor does it take place through some dramatic supernatural intervention. It is a process that demands our participation. A key element of this participation is what we have already described as the "means of grace"—activities in which we engage in response to God's gracious work in our lives. Prior to Wesley, the concept of the means of grace referred primarily to practices particularly described and commanded in the Bible: the sacraments and certain devotional practices, such as prayer and reading the Bible. Wesley expanded this idea by adding other practices. He did this in two ways that are relevant to our discussion.

Wesley added what he described as "prudential" means of grace. These activities are not explicitly taught in the Bible but, through the use of reason, Christians develop new practices from general biblical principles and discover, from experience, that they are means through which people can grow in love. One such means that Wesley promoted was "Christian conference." Wesley believed that there was great benefit in Christians meeting together, not merely for social interaction, but to reflect on their faith and their Christian living. One way Wesley promoted Christian conference, for example, was through a variety of small groups, which became key instruments in helping people grow in love. Wesley created a structure of bands, societies, and classes where Christians shared their faith and held one another accountable to regular spiritual practices. Nowhere in the Bible are we commanded to form such groups; they are developments from the biblical commands to meet together, and experience proved them to be very successful. When Methodists met together, they took time to ask one another, "And how is it with your soul?" Other inquiries included asking where people experienced the presence and grace of God in their daily lives and where they were able to serve as agents of God's grace in the lives of others. Members prayed together, reminded the whole group to pray often and to search the Holy Scriptures. There was encouragement for fasting, Christian service, and a support network through which personal needs and hardships could be addressed. In significant fashion, this defined a true community of faith. The challenge for the church in our contemporary context is not merely to repeat Wesley's innovations—though there is much to learn from them, as we will see in a later chapter—but to develop new forms that are appropriate for our times and contexts.

The second expansion of the concept of the means of grace was Wesley's addition of "works of mercy" to "works of piety"— describing both as means of grace. We might describe works of piety as religious practices. They include the sacraments, prayer, reading the Bible, fasting, and participating in communal worship. Historically, these were practices of personal piety. While Wesley encouraged acts of personal piety, it is essential to understand that Wesley's vision of "works of piety" as means of grace was corporate—or communal practices. Christians can do wonderful things individually, but together, by the power of God's Holy Spirit, they can do amazing and transformative things.

"Works of mercy" were any activities aimed at meeting the spiritual and bodily needs of other human beings. The early Methodist movement was instrumental in founding schools and universities, hospitals, orphanages, and shelters for the homeless and hungry. These were ministries that individuals could not provide individually. Only by committing to works of mercy as part of the larger movement were Methodists able to have the impact that they did. We could say that works of piety more directly express love for God, while works of mercy are the expression of love for neighbor. Here Wesley added a further development; he argued that works of mercy have priority over works of piety.

The means of grace share the following features:

- The means of grace are things we do in response to the transforming work of the Spirit. We must: read the Bible, participate in worship, and provide clothing for the needy. In doing these and other things, we express our love for God and our fellow human beings.
- The means of grace are not merely activities; the Spirit of God uses these activities to transform us so that we become more loving. Engagement in these activities reinforces and develops the inner attitudes of love for God and neighbor, which, in turn, leads to growth in outward expressions of that love.
- The means of grace are not magical procedures that automatically change us. Rather they become means of transformation through the dynamic personal interaction between the Spirit of God and the human person. Their effectiveness is dependent upon the Holy Spirit's presence and activity. Yet they are human activities, so their effectiveness is dependent upon the purpose and approach of the human participant.
- The goal of the means of grace is to transform us so that we grow in love for God and neighbor. While God can use the means of grace to transform us even when we have

wrong intentions and attitudes, they are acceptable to God only when they are used as expressions of love and means to grow in love. They are of no value when approached as self-centered goals.

Being an active member of a Christian community is an important way we can grow in holiness—not only because it is the place where we partake in communal worship, prayer, and participation in the sacraments or because we engage in communal activities to meet the needs of others—because we engage with people who are very different from us in significant ways. These differences often become a source of irritation and annoyance and can thus lead to tensions and conflicts. However, if we approach our communal life as a means of grace and see the tensions that emerge from our differences as opportunities to learn what it means to love the people who we find difficult, then participation in such a community can become a means of growing in love. In this way, the imperfections of the church can become a means of growing in love. When this happens, the public face of the church as the embodiment of divine love becomes more visible to the society around us.

Conclusion

There are four important aspects that define the church of Jesus Christ:

- First, the universal church is made up of all people transformed by the Spirit of God.
- Second, this universal church is manifest in the world in concrete communities of transformed people.

- Third, the distinguishing characteristic of these communities is that they, in various degrees, embody divine love in the world.
- Fourth, participation in communities of people transformed by the Spirit is a means God uses to further transform us.

4

WHAT DOES SUCH A CHURCH LOOK LIKE? (1)

In the last chapter, we described how the church is called to be the embodiment and cultivator of God's love in the world. In the next three chapters, we explore some of the characteristics of how the church does this with a particular focus on features that have emerged in the Wesleyan and Methodist traditions. The three characteristics that we will examine in this chapter are:

- the church as a covenant community,
- the church as a welcoming community, and
- the church as a missional community.

A Covenant Community

One of the practices John Wesley introduced into the life of early Methodism was the covenant renewal service. This service has become an important feature of Methodist church life and is often celebrated at New Year's.[1] The regular celebration of the covenant renewal service and the theology that underlies it offer important insights into Wesley's understanding of the church.

Wesley did not invent the covenant renewal service. Similar services were celebrated by British Puritans in the seventeenth century. The liturgy for the service that Wesley wrote was largely drawn from the writings of Richard Alleine (1611–1681). This is important, because it helps us understand the theological context of the idea of covenant renewal. Wesley, like the Puritans, used the concept of *covenant* to describe God's saving activity in the world through history. This, of course, has deep roots in the Bible, particularly the Old Testament. We will look briefly at a few passages from the Old Testament and then describe Wesley's understanding of the concept of *covenant*. This provides a basis to help us understand the identity and mission of the church.

Covenants in the Bible

Genesis 17:1-10 describes God entering into a covenant with Abraham:

> When Abram was 99 years old, the LORD appeared to Abram and said to him, "I am El Shaddai. Walk with me and be trustworthy. I will make a covenant between us and I will give you many, many descendants." Abram fell on his face, and God said to him, "But me, my covenant is with you; you will be the ancestor of many nations. And because I have made you the ancestor of many nations, your name will no longer be Abram but Abraham. I will make you very fertile. I will produce nations from you, and kings will come from you. I will set up my covenant with you and your descendants after you in every generation as an enduring

covenant. I will be your God and your descendants' God after you. I will give you and your descendants the land in which you are immigrants, the whole land of Canaan, as an enduring possession. And I will be their God."

God said to Abraham, "As for you, you must keep my covenant, you and your descendants in every generation. This is my covenant that you and your descendants must keep: Circumcise every male."

Let us note a few significant points:

- God makes Abram a new person: Abraham. A new identity and purpose come with the new name. God is an agent of transformation.
- God takes the initiative. Abraham does not come to God and start to bargain.
- The covenant is about a relationship. God wants to walk with Abraham and to be the most significant part of Abraham's life.
- The covenant is not only a relationship with Abraham but also with his descendants. The covenant creates a community in relationship with God.
- God makes specific promises to Abraham. Here God refers to descendants and land. These promises are part of a larger collection of promises that God makes to Abraham.
- God expects a response from Abraham. He is to walk with God, to live in the presence of God, and to be trustworthy, or, in other translations, blameless. He is to live in a relationship with God in which loyalty to God has priority over all other loyalties, and this relationship is to be expressed in his lifestyle.

- Abraham is to keep the covenant. This keeping of the covenant is ratified in the rite of circumcision, which marks Abraham and his descendants as distinct from other people. God's people are those who live in covenant with Yahweh, the God of Israel.

The concept of the covenant is expanded in the Old Testament. In particular, the revelation to Moses of the Law (see Exod 19–24) explains what faithfulness to the covenant involves in all areas of life. A further element is the warning that failure to follow the covenant will result in disaster for Israel. As the history of Israel unfolds, we discover a pattern of failure to be faithful to the covenant relationship with God: the Israelites repeatedly worship other gods and adopt a lifestyle of injustice and unrighteousness. After one such period of unfaithfulness, Josiah, king of Judah, leads a service of covenant renewal, described in 2 Kgs 23:2-3:

> Then the king went up to the Lord's temple, together with all the people of Judah and all the citizens of Jerusalem, the priests and the prophets, and all the people, young and old alike. There the king read out loud all the words of the covenant scroll that had been found in the Lord's temple. The king stood beside the pillar and made a covenant with the Lord that he would follow the Lord by keeping his commandments, his laws, and his regulations with all his heart and all his being in order to fulfill the words of this covenant that were written in this scroll. All of the people accepted the covenant.

However, such covenant renewal ceremonies did not bring about permanent change. The prophet Jeremiah looked to a day when God would radically change the people from the inside out.

The time is coming, declares the LORD, when I will make a new covenant with the people of Israel and Judah. It won't be like the covenant I made with their ancestors when I took them by the hand to lead them out of the land of Egypt. They broke that covenant with me even though I was their husband, declares the LORD. No, this is the covenant that I will make with the people of Israel after that time, declares the LORD. I will put my Instructions within them and engrave them on their hearts. I will be their God, and they will be my people. They will no longer need to teach each other to say, "Know the LORD!" because they will all know me, from the least of them to the greatest, declares the LORD; for I will forgive their wrongdoing and never again remember their sins. (Jer 31:31-34)

This prophecy envisions a new initiative from God to establish and maintain a relationship with the covenant people through inner transformation. In the New Testament, the prophecy of the new covenant is proclaimed to be fulfilled in Christ who, through work of the Spirit, brings about the promised inner transformation.

The Covenant in Wesley's Theology

The tradition of covenant theology that Wesley drew upon reflected these and other biblical passages. The first explicit reference to a covenant is found in the story of Noah and the flood, where God establishes a covenant with Noah, his descendants, and all living creatures (Gen 9). However, the basic elements of covenant relationship can be found also in the stories of Adam and Eve (Gen 2–3). The concept of the covenant became a way of describing the overarching framework of God's saving activity in the world. In summary, God's saving action *is* the covenant of grace that God enters into in the wake of the fall of Adam and Eve.

The key features of this covenant are the following:

- It is God who takes the initiative in grace to save fallen humanity.
- God requires faith as the condition of receiving forgiveness.
- God's plan for humanity is to live in relationship with them.
- The relationship from the divine side entails the promise of God's presence with and for the covenant people.
- From the human side, the relationship entails affirming divine authority over one's life and unconditional obedience.
- The covenant creates a community of those who have entered into unique relationship with God.
- Covenant takes different forms at different times; these different forms are sometimes described as *covenants* or as *dispensations*.

Wesley accepted this broad framework, though he does not discuss it in any detail. We need to note some important contributions he does make.

The first is to place the emphasis on love. Because God is love, so the foundation and goals of all of God's actions are love. The saving purpose of God is to transform creation so that it is permeated by divine love. In preparation for the new creation, God is at work to transform human beings by creating covenant communities that embody love. These, in turn, influence the broader society.

The second assertion is that, as part of this process, God teaches people what love requires. Wesley argued that all people have been

God teaches people what love requires.

given a basic understanding of what love requires, which is best understood in terms of the Golden Rule: doing unto others what you would have them do unto you. As the various dispensations and covenants unfold, so, too, does a fuller revelation of what love requires. Hence the moral requirements found in the Old Testament Law (particularly the Ten Commandments) and the Prophets are explanations of what love requires in specific relationships and contexts.

Wesley, like many other Christian thinkers, differentiated between the moral law found in the Ten Commandments and the Prophets that continue to be valid for Christians and the civil and ceremonial laws which are not. The teaching of Jesus (particularly the Sermon on the Mount) and the ethical teachings of the Epistles explain that the essence of the moral is love of God and neighbor.

The third assertion places love in the center, determining the motive and the consequences of human actions. Wesley argued that all human beings are finite and fallen, they are influenced by a host of factors, and therefore make mistakes in their understanding of the details of the moral law. What God requires is that we act out of deep love for God and our neighbors, even if we are mistaken in our understanding of what love requires. Because our understanding of love's requirements might be in error, the consequences of a particular action become an important tool for evaluation and learning. God's love is evident when our actions serve the well-being of our neighbors, while never intentionally doing harm.

The fourth assertion Wesley makes is that the use of the regular covenant renewal ceremony reinforces the idea of the church as a covenant community created by God's grace, constituted by its loyalty to the crucified Christ.

The Covenant and the Church

What does it mean for the church to be a covenant community? To answer this question, we must remember that God's love is most profoundly revealed on the cross. The broader biblical view of covenant and the role of covenant in Wesley's theology will shape our understanding, but the love of God made known on the cross is what ultimately determines the church's identity as a covenant community. Several realities about the church show that the cross is at the heart of who we are:

- The creation of the church is rooted in God's self-giving love for humanity.
- The church owes its ultimate loyalty to its crucified and resurrected Lord. All other loyalties must be subjected to this primary loyalty.
- The church expresses this loyalty in a communal lifestyle of cruciform love, that is, a love for God and humanity that is faithful, costly, self-sacrificial, other-serving, and self-debasing.
- The crucifixion disrupts and transforms all preconceived authority and leadership. Surprisingly, the lordship of Jesus the Christ is revealed in exclusion, poverty, humiliation, degradation, and the weakness of the cross. It overturns hierarchies based on power, honor, and wealth. The structures of a community in covenant with the

crucified one must reflect Jesus' voluntary and sacrificial embrace of the cross.

- Being in covenant with the crucified Christ places us in covenant with all others of the faith. Thus we are obligated to a self-sacrificial love that seeks the good of our fellow covenant members.

- Covenant commitment to Christ and to one another establishes the church as a new people of God overcoming divisions caused by race, nation, politics, and culture. People in a covenant community have a more profound unity with their fellow members than they do with others of their nation, language, class, or culture.

A Welcoming Community

The United Methodist Church has used the marketing slogan "Open Hearts, Open Minds, Open Doors," thus proclaiming itself to be a church that welcomes all. Not everyone who attends a United Methodist congregation experiences this as reality, and it challenges the church to wrestle with what it means by *open*.

My intention here is not to debate the accuracy of this United Methodist self-description, but rather to ask what the theological basis for such a description is and to explore what it means to be an "open" community of welcome.

Early Methodism as an Open Movement

Membership in early Methodism was open to all who were seeking a transforming relationship with God and gave evidence of this by doing no harm, doing good, and observing the ordinances of God (today we would say participating in the life of a worshiping community and cultivating a personal devotional life). Wesley believed that the desire for such a relationship was evidence that the Spirit was at work in people's lives, drawing them into relationship with God through Jesus Christ. This welcome was extended beyond the Methodist societies by the preachers who went into the fields, marketplaces, prisons, and wherever else people gathered to hear the message of God's love for all.

The welcoming of all, regardless of theological beliefs or denominational affiliations, was central to Wesley's understanding of Methodism. He applied this more generally to the church when he commented on Acts 11:17:

> And who are we that we should withstand God? Particularly by laying down rules of Christian communion which exclude any whom he has admitted into the Church of the first born, from worshipping God together. O that all Church governors would consider how bold an usurpation this is on the authority of the supreme Lord of the Church! O that the sin of thus withstanding God may not be laid to the charge of those, who perhaps with a good intention, but in an over fondness for their own forms, have done it, and are continually doing it.[2]

In another context, Wesley argued that the Spirit unites in one body people "who are at the greatest distance from each other by nature" (Jews and Gentiles) and "at the greatest distance by law and custom" (slaves and free persons).[3] There can be no other conditions—whether theological, ethical, cultural, racial, economic, or whatever—for full reception into the church, other than the desire for the transforming and uniting work of the Spirit.

Despite Wesley's intention and clear statements, Methodism has not always lived up to this ideal. The most obvious example in the history of The United Methodist Church is the nefarious effect of racism on the life and structures of the church. Persistent discrimination in The Methodist Episcopal Church led to Richard Allen and others leaving St. George's Methodist Episcopal Church in 1787, a move that led to the formation of The African Methodist Episcopal Church. In the aftermath of the Civil War and the emancipation of enslaved African Americans, The Methodist Episcopal Church, South, responded to the requests of its African American members by creating The Christian (then Colored) Methodist Episcopal Church, where they could worship without suffering the denigration of racist behaviors and oppression by whites. When The Methodist Episcopal Church, The Methodist Episcopal Church, South, and The Methodist Protestant Church united in 1939 to create The Methodist Church, the issue of race was a major stumbling block to the union. This was resolved by the creation of the nongeographical Central Jurisdiction for African American churches, thus entrenching segregation within the structures of the church. While the Central Jurisdiction was abolished with the creation of The United Methodist Church in 1968, racism continued to infiltrate the life of the church. It is in the light of this history that The United Methodist Church has stated in its Constitution:

> Article IV. Inclusiveness of the Church—The United Methodist Church is a part of the church universal, which is one Body in Christ. The United Methodist Church acknowledges that all persons are of sacred worth. All persons without regard to race, color, national origin, status, or economic condition, shall be eligible to attend its worship services, participate in its programs, receive the sacraments, upon baptism be admitted as baptized members, and upon taking vows declaring the Christian faith, become professing members in any local church in the connection.

In The United Methodist Church no conference or other organizational unit of the Church shall be structured so as to exclude any member or any constituent body of the Church because of race, color, national origin, status or economic condition.[4]

Today's United Methodist Church is the product of a long-standing battle to be welcoming and inclusive. United Methodists affirm John's assertion that "God so loved the world that he gave his only Son, so that everyone who believes in him won't perish but will have eternal life" (John 3:16), but they still confront sexism, racism, classism, and discrimination against the poor, the addicted, the disabled, and alternative lifestyles. To say that the church is a welcoming community is less a statement of who we are and more a description of who we seek to be.

Biblical Foundations for a Welcoming Community

We find two important biblical foundations for understanding the church as a welcoming and reconciling community in the ministry and teaching of Jesus and in Paul's theology of justification through faith. Jesus' followers included a diversity of people, many of whom simply did not belong in respectable religious society of his day: tax collectors, prostitutes, the poor, the diseased, Gentiles, and the opponents of Roman rule as well as its beneficiaries. Not only were these people his followers but he socialized with them, eating and drinking in their homes. He told parables that included the disreputable and the corrupt.

Both Jesus and Paul emphasized the importance of breaking bread together. Eating and descriptions of eating common meals together are important for two reasons. Meals in the ancient world had great symbolic value; they were seen as the physical embodiment of communion and friendship among the participants. More importantly, within Judaism, meals were often used to symbolize the coming reign of God. Having a place at the table was a promise of salvation and inclusion. In his parables, Jesus describes meals as pictures of God's coming reign and then acts them out in his habit of eating with sinners, the poor, and the rejected. His practice of welcoming these disparate people is his way of anticipating the kingdom of God. In the same way, today's church is a foretaste and anticipation of God's coming reign of love, so it to ought to be a community that welcomes and brings reconciliation among diverse, disreputable, and often-conflicted groups.

Paul called on the Romans to "welcome each other, in the same way that Christ also welcomed you" (Rom 15:7). This attitude of welcome is deeply rooted in his theology, and its significance can be seen in an incident he describes in Gal 2:11-21. He confronts Peter for no longer eating with Gentiles and describes this as not "acting consistently with the truth of the gospel" (v. 14). He goes on to explain that this is a denial of justification by faith. It might seem as if Paul overreacted. What was so significant about who ate with whom? For Paul, it was of primary significance, because table fellowship was the ultimate expression of acceptance and inclusion. When Peter withdrew from the Gentiles, he was effectively denying that they were full members of the Christian community, that they should first become Jews before they could be deemed acceptable. For Paul, it was clear that the only ground for membership in the community was God's justifying grace. By adding conditions for participation in the common meals—other than God's unconditional invitation—Peter declared it to be our actions that make us acceptable to God. Paul held that human beings should not place conditions on God's offer of salvation. A modern parallel is when racial discrimination infects the church, closing it to some people but not to others. This promotes an understanding of the gospel that requires one to be of a particular race as a condition of being part of the church, and hence of salvation.

As we read through the New Testament, we discover over and over again that it was a struggle to implement the vision of the church as a welcoming community. That struggle continues today. Clearly, being a welcoming community is not easy. In contexts where people have been deeply hurt by a church, there is a need to provide safe and healing spaces. When a church comes to the awareness that its policies and practices have been complicit, intentionally or not, in the rejection of people, there is a need for repentance and even restitution.

> *God's love, grace, mercy, and compassion must become our own; only when we open ourselves to true and full transformation will we ever realize this vision of inclusivity.*

It is a huge challenge and demands a great level of maturity for those who have been hurt to be willing to accept those who do them harm. It is equally daunting to expect people who hold very strong beliefs about righteous and unrighteous behavior to be comfortable with those they feel are behaving in unfaithful or even sinful ways. There is no simple approach to address such a complex situation. Cultivating tolerance, civility, mutual respect, and empathy can be accomplished only by the power of God's Holy Spirit. God's love, grace, mercy, and compassion must become our own; only when we open ourselves to true and full transformation will we ever realize this vision of inclusivity.

A Missional Community

Mission was at the core of early Methodism—quite simply it existed for mission. It was not so much that Methodism had a mission; it was a mission in the world. The same is true of the church. It is not so much that the church has a mission; it is a mission. Serving the world, those outside the church in a wide variety of neediness and want, has consistently defined the Methodist purpose. In every age, United Methodism and its component denominations (The Evangelical Association, United Brethren in Christ, The Methodist/Methodist Episcopal/Methodist Episcopal, South) have defined themselves by their mission. As the community that embodies divine love in the world in the anticipation of the final triumph of love, our mission is God's mission in the world. We fulfill our identity when we serve those who are outside the community.

Wesley's Understanding of Mission

Early Methodism in Britain and America had a clear sense of mission, which was combined with passion, practical strategies, and flexible institutional structures, and which resulted in substantial growth and made a major impact on the broader society. This raises the question of how the early Methodists understood mission. In a number of places, Wesley describes what he understands the mission of Methodism to be. I have selected four examples that we will examine and use as a basis for developing a Methodist understanding of mission. It is noteworthy that each uses very different language and offers a unique focus; yet, at the same time, a central thread runs through them all. The statements are:

- Reform the nation, and in particular the Church, to spread scriptural holiness over the land.[5]
- We unite together for this and no other end— to promote, as far as we are capable, justice, mercy, and truth, the glory of God, and peace and goodwill among men.[6]
- Do nothing but save souls.[7]
- Offer them Christ.[8]

Reform the nation, and in particular the Church, to spread scriptural holiness over the land.

Wesley was deeply disturbed by the political and social climate in Britain in his day. There was corruption in all levels of government. There was a vast wealth gap and high levels of poverty. Crime was widespread, and the cruel punishments imposed on offenders brutalized society. The socially deprived took solace in cheap liquor and gambling. Standards of public morality were low. Despite the official status of the Church of England, there was a general disregard for religion. The health of the church of that time is best described as mixed. While there were faithful clergy, there were also corrupt, negligent, and abusive pastoral leaders. Wesley was convinced that the mission of Methodism was to reform the nation and the church. For many of us the word *reform* carries implications of structural, institutional, or legal change. Wesley's

> *A holy life is one in which love permeates all its dimensions, and it results in action to transform society.*

focus was elsewhere. For him reform had to be deeper; it had to transform the human heart. Thus, the key to the reform of the nation and the church was in spreading "scriptural holiness over the land." However, this was not a withdrawal from society or a retreat into personal piety. Genuine holiness of heart is manifest in holiness of life. A holy life is one in which love permeates all its dimensions, and it results in action to transform society. It is important to note that Wesley did not define *holiness* in terms of doctrine and polity, but as a basic integration of thought, word, and deed.

We unite together for this and no other end—to promote, as far as we are capable, justice, mercy, and truth, the glory of God, and peace and goodwill among men.

This statement comes from a letter to King George II at a time of political uncertainty in Britain, and Wesley was concerned to express the loyalty of Methodists to the king. On the advice of others, he did not actually send it to the king. As we have already seen, the triad of justice, mercy, and truth often appears in Wesley's writings as a way of summarizing outward love for one's neighbors, or, more particularly, of doing unto others as one would have them do unto you. *Justice* refers to treating people with the value and dignity they have as human beings and evaluating their actions fairly. *Mercy* goes beyond justice and seeks, on the one hand, to meet the needs of suffering and deprived human beings; and on the other, a deep empathy that seeks to understand who people are and what they do from within their own life situations. It forces Christians to treat others by a standard beyond what others deserve. We do not treat others as they deserve, but by the guidance of the Golden Rule. *Truth* includes being truthful in what one states, but goes beyond that to integrity and faithfulness in all areas of life.

What is interesting about this triad is how Wesley applies it to all dimensions of human life. He expects that, as a consequence of prevenient grace, it will be found among those who are not Christians. Justice, mercy, and truth are evidence that all people are created in the image of God, whether they have acknowledged God or accepted the faith. Justice, mercy, and truth are universal. In some places, Wesley positively contrasts societies in Asia and Africa with those in Europe, because they show greater evidence of justice, mercy, and truth. If Methodists are to pursue justice, mercy, and truth, they will have to engage not only people's personal lives but also the communal, social, political, and economic dimensions of human life. Today, many Christians claim that we should keep politics and religion separate; for Wesley, this would be a ridiculous impossibility. To live our faith in the world impacts all aspects: education, economics, politics, associations, involvement in the community, and our loyalties to state and nation. Promoting the glory of God is a comprehensive statement that is best described as working to bring about a situation where human life is permeated by a love for God and all people. Promoting peace and good will is working for the improvement of the spiritual and bodily well-being of all people. In a context of political turmoil, Wesley understood our obligation as working for peace and stability in society. Given Wesley's intention of expressing loyalty to the king, he evidently did not think that this comprehensive mission was a threat or challenge to the sociopolitical order of his day. It did, however, become so later in his life, when it led to his active engagement to end the slave trade that was a key foundation of British economic success.

Do nothing but save souls.

The phrase to "save souls" has become synonymous with evangelism and in contemporary society often conveys the impression of a very other-worldly and socially irrelevant understanding of the mission of the church; a focus on ensuring that people "go to heaven" when they die. Clearly, when Wesley referred to saving souls, he was referring to evangelism; this did include the concept of people gaining an assurance of life with God after death. This was central to his ministry. However, this was not a simplistic calling of people to a profession of faith; it was calling people into a transforming relationship with God that began with the first steps of faith and led to a new life and lifestyle consummated in the presence of God. A soul that was saved was one that had been transformed into the image of God, resulting in a life permeated by God's love. This was not a one-time event, but a lifelong process of transformation.

Offer them Christ.

When Wesley used the phrase "offer them Christ," it signified introducing people to the threefold office of Christ: prophet, priest, and king. As prophet, Christ announces the moral law of God's love, teaches us how this law should shape all dimensions of our lives, and shows us the ways we have failed to stay in faithful covenant. As priest, Christ brings forgiveness of sins and reconciles us to God. As king, Christ rules and transforms us so that we manifest holiness of heart and life—in the terminology we have been using—so that we are permeated by divine love.

Wesley's understanding of mission is comprehensive and integrated. Clearly, evangelism as the invitation into a transforming relationship with God is at the core. However, this does not exclude a broader engagement with people's personal, communal, social, economic, and political lives. Evangelism is complete only when it results in people who are actively engaged in meeting the needs of others through lives committed to justice, mercy, and truth.

With Wesley and Beyond Wesley: Mission Today

Contemporary contexts are different from Wesley's culture, and the Methodist movement has developed since Wesley's day in many different directions. Throughout the years, different aspects of Wesley's understanding of mission have been emphasized. Today, we need to recover the integrated and comprehensive understanding of mission Wesley taught, putting it in a current theological context in a way that is consistent with Wesley's writings. For Wesley, the church is called to be the community that embodies divine love in a broken world, thus anticipating the final fulfillment of God's purpose, when human society and all creation will be permeated by divine love. As such a community, the church serves those outside the church and becomes a source of renewal and transformation in society.

What, then, is mission for our day? It is bearing witness to the transforming love of God through word, presence, and action. The church is called to proclaim the good news that God is active in the world, establishing the divine reign of love inaugurated in the life, death, and resurrection of Christ. We live this reality now as we await the consummation of the new heaven and the new earth. With this goes the amazing offer that God gives to human beings.

> *What, then, is mission for our day?*
> *It is bearing witness to the*
> *transforming love of God through*
> *word, presence, and action.*

God wants us to participate in this reign of love through a personal transformative relationship with God's very self through Christ, by the work of the Spirit. God's reign is erupting into the world in communities of people transformed by the love of God. This verbal message has no credibility if there are no communities that embody God's reign of love. Hence, the presence of communities of people whose personal lives have been transformed and whose communal life is permeated by divine love are integral to the witness of what God is doing. In an increasingly secular age, where all "God talk" is suspect, the authenticity of the message must be validated by the reality of transformed communities. Finally, all talk of love carries no meaning unless it is concretely expressed in meeting the needs of others. Such action to meet the needs of others ranges from the personal through the communal to the social and political.

Reflection

If mission was central to early Methodism, then mission is central to United Methodism today. In a context of uncertainty and threat, The United Methodist Church denies its own reason for existence when it focuses on self or institutional preservation rather than on mission. The challenge before us today is how we make mission central to the life of The United Methodist Church as a whole.

Can we reenvision *church* to be a network of local congregations that are committed to being the expression of the love of God in society, calling others to share in God's transformative mission?

Conclusion

In this chapter, we have examined three themes: the church as a covenant community, the church as a welcoming community, and the church as a missional community. It is important to see that these three themes are integrated, one with the other. The church is constituted as a community by its covenantal relationship with the crucified Christ. As the covenant community, it is open to all who are in relationship with Christ and expresses God's gracious welcome to all. The covenant is the description of God's activity to transform people in community so that they are permeated by divine love. The covenant community is thus called into mission, to be the embodiment and agent of divine love in the world.

5

WHAT DOES SUCH A CHURCH LOOK LIKE? (2)

This chapter continues to examine characteristics of the church that are significant within the Methodist tradition. We start by looking at the church as sacramental community, a church that regularly gathers to celebrate Holy Communion. When the church places the remembrance of Christ's sacrifice at the center of its life, this gives rise to a transformed way of life so that the church becomes a countercultural community. However, maintaining a countercultural ethos is not easy, and the temptation to conform to the dominant values of a given society is strong. The countercultural ethos can be maintained and grow only when the church is a community of mutual accountability and support.

A Sacramental Community

Early Methodism can be described in many ways. For some it was primarily an evangelistic movement, for others a holiness movement, while for others it was a movement of social reform. All of these are true to varying degrees, and it must also be added that it was a movement for sacramental renewal, which placed the celebration of Holy Communion in the center of the Christian life. From his student days in Oxford, Wesley practiced a regular participation in Holy Communion. During his life, it is estimated that he celebrated Communion on average about once every five days. He published a collection of hymns written by himself and his brother Charles that were specifically to be used in the celebration of Holy Communion. At the end of his life, it was the need for American Methodists to have access to Communion that led him to ordain preachers to administer the sacraments, contrary to the rules of the Church of England. Wesley's expectation was that a worshiping community would celebrate the sacrament of the Lord's Supper every time they met together under the guidance of an ordained clergyperson. In this section, we will explore Wesley's understanding of Holy Communion and its significance for the life and mission of the church.

Holy Communion in John Wesley's Theology

Holy Communion is of central significance in Wesley's understanding of the Christian life and in his own spiritual life, because he regarded it as a primary means of grace through which we are transformed by divine love. Over the centuries, Christian thinkers have debated the meaning, practice, institution, and effect of Holy Communion. These debates led to conflicts and divisions within the church. Even in our contemporary context, differences in interpreting and understanding Holy Communion are a major point of contention between the Roman Catholic and Protestant churches. In briefly explaining some significant features of

Wesley's interpretation of Holy Communion, the intention is not to enter into debate and conflict with others, but to examine how Wesley contributes to a fuller understanding of the Communion experience. Here, as in other aspects of his theology, Wesley made use of ideas from others.

> ## *In eating the bread and drinking from the cup, we meet with Jesus Christ through the work of the Spirit.*

The first important aspect of Wesley's theology of Communion is that it is communion with Christ. In eating the bread and drinking from the cup, we meet with Jesus Christ through the work of the Spirit. Celebrating Communion is not merely the participation in religious ritual; even less is it a quasi-magical event. It is the meeting with the one who loves us, who gave himself for us, who desires to live in relationship with us, who forgives us, who engages with us to liberate us from our self-centeredness, and who transforms us so that our lives may become permeated by love.

A second aspect is that the focus of Communion is the re-presentation of the crucifixion of Christ. The death of Christ is symbolically made present to the congregation. As we noted in the last chapter, every encounter with Christ is an encounter with him in all his offices—as priest, prophet, and king; this is also true of the representation of the death of Christ. As priest, the representation of the crucified Christ is the enacted proclamation of God's forgiving, accepting, and adopting love. As prophet, it is the enacted proclamation of the divine purpose that we live lives of cruciform love for God and our fellows. As king, the representation of the crucified Christ is a means of grace that transforms us so that our lives become increasingly permeated by divine love.

A third aspect for Wesley is that Holy Communion is a converting ordinance. Participation in Communion is a means through which God transforms us, increases our faith, and redirects our lives into covenant loyalty to the crucified Christ. It is important to note two implications of this. The first is that all are welcome to the table who wish to enter or grow in a transforming relationship with God. The desire to enter such a relationship is a demonstration of incipient faith, and participation in Communion is a means through which that faith can grow and develop. The second is that regular, faith-filled participation in Communion will lead to growth in one's relationship with God.

A fourth aspect is that Wesley's understanding of Communion is corporate. While there is a strong focus on the individual person's encounter with Christ, many of the hymns written by John and Charles Wesley for Communion use plural pronouns. "We" as a body come to the table to commune with the living Christ. No individual believer may celebrate the sacrament alone; this is first and foremost a communal act.

The final aspect that I will comment on is that Communion has a future focus. The encounter with the crucified Christ points us forward to the goal of the Christian life in the fullness of God's presence and the goal of fulfillment in the new creation. It thus points to the ultimate goal of creation, when the presence of the God of love will so transform the world that it becomes permeated by the love of God.

Communion as the Enactment of Open Community

Let us briefly jump over two centuries from Wesley and to another continent. The year is 1982, the place Cape Town, South Africa. An Anglican priest named Harry Wiggett is asked to act as chaplain to the political prisoners in Pollsmoor prison; among these prisoners is the lifelong Methodist Nelson Mandela. Wiggett celebrated Communion with the prisoners as often as he could. In his book, *A Time to Speak,*[1] Wiggett describes the first Communion service. A few prisoners gathered around the Communion table; at the side of the room observing the proceedings to ensure nothing "suspicious" took place was a prison warder, Christo Brand. Wiggett began the liturgy, and the gathering had just shared the peace when Mandela interrupted, asking him to stop; Mandela then walked over to Christo Brand and asked him if he was a Christian. Brand replied that he was. Mandela said: "Well then…join us round this table. You cannot sit apart. This is Holy Communion, and we must share and receive it together."[2] The warder drew his chair to the table, and together with the prisoners, shared in the Communion.

This scene profoundly enacts some important developments in Methodist theology after Wesley. The first is a deepening appreciation of the universal, communal character of Communion. Noted above is the fact that Wesley used plural pronouns to indicate that Communion is a corporate meeting with the crucified Lord. Missing, however, is an emphasis, found in the New Testament, that Holy Communion is not only communion with Christ but also with others as members of the body of Christ. In the early church, the more ritualized taking of the bread and the cup took place within the context of a communal meal. The Christians came

> ***Holy Communion is not only communion with Christ but also with others as members of the body of Christ.***

together, shared their food, and reclined at the table in close physical proximity (reclining involves bodily nearness, even contact). This intense intimacy gains deeper significance when we recognize that the membership of these early Christian communities transcended the social and cultural barriers and divisions of the time. To participate in Communion is to symbolically embody what it means to be a new community, united by our common relationship with the resurrected crucified one.

Tragically, the church often fails to do this. In early American Methodism, the practice arose that required African Americans to sit in a separate part of the church, and to serve them Communion last. The presence of black bodies was not acceptable to white members in general, and in particular, the practice of white members drinking from the same cup and eating from the same plate that had been used by African American members was to be avoided. This stands in stark contrast to the intention of the sacrament. Communion is a sign of our mutual love and community with one another. On a local level, Communion witnesses to our willingness to be one with all people in Christ. On a global level, our love and community extends beyond those who are physically present to embrace all Christians across the world. As such, it expresses our unity in Christ and ought to motivate us to strive for fuller expressions of this unity.

The second development was the practice of open Communion, which emerged from Wesley's understanding of Communion as a converting ordinance. Open Communion is the practice of giving an open invitation to all who are seeking Christ to come to the table. Within The United Methodist Church, this goes to the extent of opening the table to those who are not baptized, though it recognizes that baptism is the normal prerequisite for membership in the church community. The celebration of Holy Communion is not a secret ritual for the initiated, but may be the means by which God's grace is first received by an uninitiated seeker.

The third development is the missional dimension. Having encountered the transforming presence of Christ at the table, we are sent out into the world to manifest cruciform love to those outside the church—through our words, our presence, and our concrete acts of justice and mercy. Our common liturgy states that through the Eucharist, we are made one with Christ, one with each other, and one in ministry to all the world. These are not separate characteristics, but three facets of one reality. The common union (communion) we experience unites us to God by the power of the Holy Spirit to function together as the incarnate body of Christ in the world. This is an elegant marriage of works of piety and works of mercy.

Let us return to the story with which we began this section. A Methodist layperson, a prisoner who was oppressed and discriminated against, invited the person whose presence and work embodied the oppressive and racist state to join him at the Communion table. It was an act that radically reversed the social order, embodied divine love, and created a new community in the midst of everything that would deny it. This is a profound illustration of Holy Communion as the means to an open, inclusive, healing, and missional community.

A Countercultural Community

Once, when visiting the United States for some church meetings, I was waiting in a long line to get to the immigration offices. I was tired after the long flight and just wanted to get out and to my hotel as soon as possible. It seemed to take such a long time for the person in front of me to be processed, and I wondered whether I would also face many detailed questions. When my turn came, the officer asked me why I was coming to the US. I replied that I worked for The United Methodist Church and was attending church meetings. He responded, "Beautiful," stamped my passport, and I was on my way. Being a United Methodist in the US is socially respectable, and in some cases, as in this one, it has advantages. This is not the case everywhere. Where I live in Switzerland, this is not always the case. Here, when one popular politician and member of the *Nationalrat*—the Swiss equivalent of the House of Representatives—comes up for reelection, there are questions and discussion in the press about his strange religion and its possible impact on his political decisions. He is a Methodist.

Early Methodism, like United Methodism in some parts of the world today, was not considered to be socially respectable. *Methodist* was originally a derogatory term for a small splinter group of Anglicans who followed a narrow and restrictive discipline. Being a Methodist carried no social or economic advantages. Methodists were regarded as religious fanatics and became the objects of satirical cartoons. They were looked down upon, and becoming a Methodist meant stepping out of popular society. It must be noted that this prejudice was merely the consequence of Methodists deliberately adopting a way of life that stood in contrast to what many considered to be socially acceptable, particularly among the more well-to-do classes. To be a Methodist was to be part of a countercultural movement.

If United Methodism is to be true to its roots, it will increasingly return to its countercultural heritage. Being countercultural means different things in different sociocultural contexts. This is true not only from country to country but also place to place, and region to region within a country. In the United States, being Democrat in a predominantly Republican area is countercultural, but the same is also true of being a Republican in a region populated by Democrats. Being a United Methodist should be countercultural in both political regions.

> *If United Methodism is to be true to its roots, it will increasingly return to its countercultural heritage.*

Community of the Crucified

Early Christian communities gathered on a regular basis to eat a common meal, and, as part of this meal, they engaged in a ritual of eating bread and drinking wine in memory of Jesus' death. This ritual eating and drinking has become so much part of our culture that we no longer realize how shocking it would have been in first-century Greco-Roman culture. Eating common meals was a regular part of the life of many associations of the time, both religious and secular. The communal dynamics of the common meal (including seating arrangements, types of food, and who ate what food) were a concrete manifestation of the ideals and beliefs of the association responsible for the meal. What would have horrified the broader society in the first century was that at the center of this meal was a symbolic reenactment of the death of one who was executed as a criminal, represented as blood and body in wine and bread. Moreover, the manner of this execution was an appalling issue. Crucifixion was the manner of execution reserved for the "scum" of society: slaves, rebels, insurrectionists, and traitors. It was a torturously painful death accompanied by mockery, exclusion, degradation, and shame. Jewish tradition further interpreted crucifixion as a sign of being under a divine curse. Jesus was rejected by the religious and political elite of his people, and handed over to the enemies of the Jewish people to be stripped naked (the ultimate expression of shame), tortured, killed, and thus put under a divine curse. He was crucified with two others, symbolically identifying him with the degraded, the shamed, the criminal, and the condemned. It was an incredible and risky act when Christians made this the center of their common meal and their identity. They went beyond this, proclaiming that God raised this Jesus from the dead and that he was the true Savior and Lord of the world. *Savior* and *Lord* were titles usually ascribed to the Roman emperor. But Christians identified the ultimate emperor as the one who had been degraded and executed by Rome. The Communion meal focused on the crucifixion and resurrection of Jesus as the key to understanding who God is and the purpose of human life.

In many ways, the entire New Testament is an explanation of God's nature and will and of God's purpose for our lives. It would take far more than one brief section in this book to do justice to the scope and range of these teachings. For our purposes, it is of utmost priority to recognize the cross of Christ as that which defines the nature of love of which we speak. Christian love is cruciform love. There are five points that ground this premise:

- The cross redefines greatness; the greatness of God is revealed in the degradation and agony of the cross and not in imperial pomp and triumph.
- The cross reveals divine love as demanding, costly, self-sacrificial, and self-debasing.
- The cross calls for ultimate and unequivocal loyalty to the crucified Lord.
- The cross reveals service, and not domination and imposition, as the mode of Christian engagement in the world.
- The cross reveals God as the one who is present with—and who identifies God's very self with—the rejected, the shamed, the degraded, the disempowered, the victims, and the suffering.

These five points, along with many others, should shape the communal ethos and identity of those who gather regularly around the table to eat from the loaf and drink from the cup in memory of Jesus the Christ.

Countercultural Methodism

While John Wesley did not expound the significance of the cross in precisely the way I have done here, we can find aspects of this throughout his theology. He was also concerned to constitute Methodism as a countercultural community shaped by divine love. Wesley envisioned a community that had the mind of Christ—a phrase taken from Phil 2:5 (NRSV), where Paul relates it directly to the crucifixion—and walked as Christ did, the way of the cross. Wesley attempted to explain what divine love required in the eighteenth century by drawing up his General Rules, which all Methodists were expected to accept and follow.[3] These rules delineated the contours of a countercultural lifestyle in the context of eighteenth-century Britain, thus establishing Methodism as a countercultural community seeking and experiencing a transforming relationship with God.

Wesley divided the rules into three categories: Do no harm. Do good to all. Attend on the ordinances of God. (We would probably say today something like participating in practice of individual and communal devotion and worship.) These are outward and visible expressions of divine love. The first two express love for all human beings, and the latter expresses love for God.

When we examine the General Rules, we do not find a comprehensive list of beliefs and practices, but broad categories that help us understand how we might better live in loving covenant community. A few examples will demonstrate this.

Wesley taught that Methodists should not buy or sell goods on which import duties have not been paid. Smuggling was a way of life in parts of Wesley's Britain, particularly in Cornwall where Methodism experienced significant growth. Wesley was convinced that Christians had a duty to pay taxes, not least because the failure to do so increased the burden on those who could least afford it— the poor. To refrain from smuggling was in the context a major countercultural stand and one that Wesley struggled to implement.

In a context of considerable poverty and deprivation, the rule to do good to people's "bodies, of the ability which God giveth, by giving food to the hungry, by clothing the naked, by visiting or helping them that are sick or in prison" was not only a significant expression of loving one's neighbor; it also caused considerable offense in middle-class society. It was a common belief that poor people were receiving exactly what they deserved from life. The idea that those with means had any kind of responsibility for those without was not easily or widely accepted.

There is one significant change added by the American Methodists to John Wesley's original list: the rejection of "Slaveholding; buying or selling slaves." While combating slavery and the slave trade became a significant issue for Wesley toward the end of his life, there was very little actual slavery in Britain. Hence, it was not the issue for British Methodists that it was for American Methodists and was thus added to the General Rules in America.

Being Countercultural Today

Within The United Methodist Church, the General Rules are prevented, by our Constitution, from being changed or revoked, except by a supermajority of all members of all annual conferences in the denomination. While this might serve an important role in preserving the General Rules as a historic artifact of our Methodist heritage, an unintended consequence is that we too easily dismiss them as responses to specific issues in eighteenth-century societies, and therefore, wrongly consider them irrelevant today. The truth is that there may never have been a more critical time in our history to reflect deeply on what it means to do no harm, to do all the good we can, and to engage in those practices that give us our unique identity in Christ. Not doing harm, doing good, and growing in faith-focused, love-saturated discipleship may be the most countercultural witness we can possibly offer.

> *Not doing harm, doing good,*
> *and growing in faith-focused,*
> *love-saturated discipleship may*
> *be the most countercultural witness*
> *we can possibly offer.*

It is imperative that we take as our starting point divine love revealed on the cross, and that we grapple with what it means in our modern contexts to do no harm, to do good, and to attend upon the ordinances of God. In doing so, we should note the following:

- In different contexts there will be different points where the The United Methodist Church needs to take a countercultural stand; the General Rules will be lived out differently in different contexts.
- Countercultural rules will be controversial even within our church and therefore need to be carefully grounded in God's revelation in Christ.
- While the practice of countercultural rules are context-specific, it sometimes occurs that people from outside a context can see the issues clearer than those within it; there is a need to listen to the voices of people in other contexts.
- Being countercultural is costly and can lead to significant opposition.
- There is a need for a certain degree of flexibility in allowing for different responses to particular issues that are consistent with cruciform love.

A Community of Mutual Accountability

Methodism, in calling for holiness of heart and life, was a rejection of nominal, passive Christianity—a Christianity in which people were part of the church in name, but not in the living of their daily lives. Wesley taught that to be a Christian was to live a countercultural life permeated by cruciform love. Living such a countercultural life is not easy. We struggle against our own self-centeredness—our sin—and the pressure of societies that embody and promote values and ways of life that are contrary to God's revelation in the crucified Christ. John Wesley noted how often a revival preacher would evangelize in an area and have great success, but after he had left, people quickly returned to their old ways of life. Wesley's answer to the problem of people failing to continue and to grow in their Christian life was to develop a network of small groups: bands, classes, and select societies.

Theology of Small Groups

As a faithful Anglican, John Wesley never forgot the importance and centrality of corporate worship and congregational life. However, Wesley also realized that growth in the Christian life required more than weekly worship. What was missing for Wesley was an intimate, focused accountability directed toward daily living. In small groups, Wesley believed that authentic Christian living and continuous spiritual growth would result. While Wesley's small groups grew as pragmatic responses to particular situations, he felt small groups were the best way to address key theological concerns:

- Sin remains within believers, distorting our motives and turning us away from God and others.

- God's grace empowers us to overcome sin and live a life of love for God and others.
- God's grace usually works through means, that is, human activities in which we must participate.
- One of the key ways in which God works is to bring us into community with other Christians.
- We have a duty to love our siblings in Christ, and an important element of this love is to facilitate their spiritual growth by encouragement and warning.
- Christianity is not a solitary religion. How we live has an impact on the life of our siblings in Christ and on the health and witness of the church.

Wesleyan Small Groups in Practice

Each of the small groups Wesley developed—*classes, bands,* and *select societies*—had specific functions within his understanding of the Christian life.

Classes were the basic unit of early Methodism and were open to all who sought a transforming relationship with God. They were organized geographically and included women and men. The leader of the class could be male or female. They were held on a weekly basis, and regular participation in class was a condition of membership in the local Methodist Society (congregation).

Bands were for those who had experienced the new birth and were seeking to grow in their experience of God's transforming work. In Wesleyan terminology, they were for those "going on to perfection." By *perfection,* Wesley meant a further experience of God's transforming work that resulted in a life permeated and dominated by love. Bands were organized in such a way as to promote homogeneity in areas such as gender, marital status, and age. The aim was to enable a greater level of intimacy and mutual vulnerability.

Select societies were for those who had experienced Christian perfection and were seeking to continue to flourish in their lives of love.

Despite their differences, these groups had a similar function: to provide a context of mutual accountability and support in living a countercultural lifestyle permeated by divine love. While a group would pray together and sing hymns, the focus was on asking one another about spiritual life. In the classes, the General Rules played an important function as a way of measuring the extent to which one was living a life of love. However, the groups were about much more than keeping rules. They were places where people could share in complete confidence their struggles, difficulties, and successes. Here people could find support, but could also be challenged in their ongoing attempts to embody God's love in the world. In an often-hostile environment, these groups were the source of strength in Methodism, promoting spiritual growth and practical Christian living.

It is important to note two other issues. An important part of the class meetings was the collection of money to provide for the poor. This provided a practical way of expressing love in the world. In the select societies, this was taken a step further, and the members were encouraged to develop a community of property, following the example of the early church in Jerusalem. Community was not merely spiritual, but also practical.

Small Groups Today

While the network of small groups was a great source of strength in early Methodism, in most parts of the Methodist family of churches they have fallen into decline and, in some cases, have disappeared altogether. Some scholars trace the decline of the Methodist movement to the disappearance of these groups. They have sometimes been replaced by other forms of small groups, but these often have not focused on mutual spiritual accountability. One of the signs of a renewal within United Methodism in recent years has been a rediscovery of Wesleyan small groups for accountable discipleship. A number of books have been written seeking to develop contemporary models for mutual accountability groups, and they are worth looking into.[4]

If United Methodist churches are to be networks of communities that embody and share God's transforming cruciform love, then there is a need to develop a culture of mutual accountability and responsibility that nurtures and encourages growth in embodying God's love. The implementation of such groups raises significant issues. In some contemporary contexts, several of Wesley's methods appear to be an unwanted intrusion into people's personal lives. Modern culture in the United States is highly individualistic, personal, and private. Many people today feel their relationship with God is no one's business but their own. Accountability holds little attraction or value for many Christians, and there is even some suspicion about the integrity of accountability processes. While accountability groups can be a place of growth, they can also become manipulative, oppressive, sectarian, and coercive. There is a need to develop group practices that promote the flourishing of life and responsible living. Space must be provided for a diversity of ways of embodying cruciform love, allowing for a genuine freedom of conscience. At their best, such groups can provide a space for the members to be mutually accountable to one another, to be supportive of one another, and to work out together what the love of God and neighbor demands.

Conclusion

The charge to become a community permeated by cruciform love is daunting. It might seem impossible to some. However, in contexts of increasing secularization, where all forms of God talk—particularly that associated with organized religion—are regarded with suspicion, Christian communities must provide an alternative. Without such a witness of love, our words ring hollow, and our mission will fail. However, the three dimensions of the church discussed in this chapter provide some key insights into how we can cultivate such communities. They are: (1) to be a people defined by our celebration of Communion, (2) to be committed to a countercultural witness of inclusion and grace, and (3) to connect in small groups for accountability and support. These dimensions challenge us to work out contextually what it means to be the community of divine love. We can begin to embody this as we become communities of mutual responsibility and accountability.

6

WHAT DOES SUCH A CHURCH LOOK LIKE? (3)

The previous two chapters explored some characteristics of the church that arose from our Methodist heritage. In this chapter, we will look at three more: the church as a community on the margins, the church as a connectional community, and the church as a transnational community.

Community on the Margins

Chapter 5 proposed that a typical characteristic of the church is that it is a countercultural community whose identity is constituted by its confession that Jesus Christ is the Lord who calls his followers to a life of cruciform love in the world. This section explores further what it means to be a countercultural community by exploring the relationship between the church, as the body of the crucified one, and people who are rejected, abandoned, deprived, and exploited by our societies.

> *The church is called to embody Christ's love to all, especially to those who are most vulnerable in our world.*

Within all the contexts in which we live, there are people who experience deprivation, exclusion, and exploitation—people who live on the margins of our societies and even our churches. Life on the margins may be a result of numerous economic, cultural, political, and even religious factors. People living in the mainstream of society or a particular community may take little time to consider those who live on the margins, those for whom life may be a daily struggle or a source of shame and degradation. Yet the church is called to embody Christ's love to all, especially to those who are most vulnerable in our world.

Insights from Wesley

Methodists often celebrate Wesley's Aldersgate experience—when he felt his heart being "strangely warmed" as he came to an assurance that he did truly trust in Christ alone for his salvation and that his sins had been forgiven—as the decisive event in the emergence of Methodism. However, a possibly equally important event happened a year later, when Wesley, at the invitation of George Whitefield, began preaching in the open air to impoverished workers in a Bristol brickyard. In his *Journals*, he describes it as follows:

> At four in the afternoon I submitted to "being more vile" and proclaimed the glad tidings of salvation . . . in a ground adjoining the city. . . . The Scripture on which I spoke was this (is it possible anyone should be ignorant that it is fulfilled in

every true minister of Christ?): "The Spirit of the Lord is upon me, because he has anointed me to preach the gospel to the poor. He hath sent me to heal the broken-hearted, to preach deliverance to the captives and recovery of sight to the blind, to set at liberty them that are bruised, and to proclaim the acceptable year of the Lord."[1]

Engagement with the poor and despised members of society was part of Wesley's life and ministry from his student days at Oxford, where he provided for the hungry, visited prisoners, educated poor children, and engaged in other works of mercy. Yet the movement into the fields marked a new direction of leaving "respectable society" and identifying with those he elsewhere describes as the "outcasts of men." The message of both John and Charles Wesley was well-received by those who were deprived, exploited, and rejected by "respectable society." Much later in his life, John Wesley took up the cause of enslaved Africans. Their suffering was the foundation of British economic growth and a significant source of the wealth of the city of Bristol, which had become a major center for Methodism. For Wesley, these were not mere acts of charity toward the poor, but a lifestyle of solidarity with and on behalf of the poor and the excluded. He adopted a frugal lifestyle: he went as far as begging on behalf of the poor; when he was in London, he ate with the poor who were being fed by Methodists; he visited the poor, the sick, and the prisoners, putting his own health and well-being at risk. More than that, he instructed the early Methodists to adopt a similar lifestyle. This focus on the poor and the welcome reception that Wesley received from the poor contributed to the opposition that he encountered from within and beyond the church. What is of particular interest is the way he related this to the central themes of his message.

In the General Rules, under the theme of doing good, he calls Methodists to take "up their cross daily; submitting to bear the reproach of Christ, to be as the filth and offscouring of the world; and looking that men should say all manner of evil of them *falsely*, for the Lord's sake."[2] In a number of other places, he described the Christian life in a similar way. The phrase "filth and offscouring of the world" comes from 1 Cor 4:13 (King James Version), which the Common English Bible translates as "We have become the scum of the earth, the waste that runs off everything." For Wesley, following Christ entailed taking a path toward rejection and exclusion; it meant moving to the margins of society.

Wesley believed that when the church fell to the temptation to move toward the centers of power and wealth in society, it would result in corruption and demise. We can see this in his sermon "The Mystery of Iniquity," where he stated:

> Persecution never did, never could, give any lasting wound to genuine Christianity. But the greatest it ever received, the grand blow which was struck at the very root of that humble, gentle, patient love, which is the fulfilling of the Christian law, the whole essence of true religion, was struck in the fourth century by Constantine the Great, when he called himself a Christian, and poured in a flood of riches, honours, and power upon the Christians; more especially upon the Clergy.[3]

Integral to taking up one's cross—or to use Wesley's other favorite language, having the mind of Christ so that we might walk as he did—is a lifestyle of ministry with, and action on behalf of, the deprived and rejected. Charles Wesley expressed this in a poem:

> The poor as Jesus' bosom-friends,
>> The poor he makes his latest care,

> To all his successors commends,
>   And wills us on our hands to bear:
> The poor our dearest care we make,
>   Aspiring to superior bliss,
> And cherish for their Saviour's sake,
>   And love them with a love like his.[4]

John Wesley explicitly argued in a number of his writings that the life of holiness required those following Christ to be among the poor, the suffering, the uneducated, the widows, and the orphans. In a series of letters to Miss J. C. March, an educated and wealthy woman, he urged her to visit the poor. In one letter from February 1776, he wrote: "Creep in among these in spite of dirt and an hundred disgusting circumstances, and thus put off the gentlewoman. Do not confine your conversation to genteel and elegant people."[5] The word *conversation* here is probably to be understood in the broader eighteenth-century sense of social interaction. In the light of this, we can argue that engagement in ministry with, for, and on behalf of those whom society discriminates against, excludes, exploits, and oppresses is a characteristic feature of Methodist identity.

Jesus on the Margins

We noted that for John and Charles Wesley this engagement with people who were rejected, deprived, and excluded was an aspect of what it meant to have the mind of Christ and to walk as he did. The Wesley brothers' insights can be deepened by looking briefly at the life of Christ.

The accounts of Jesus' birth place him among the excluded and marginalized. He is conceived by an unmarried young woman, and thus, from the time of Mary's pregnancy, he was identified with the socially unacceptable. Luke describes how his parents are forced to travel—at a completely inappropriate and undesirable time for a pregnant woman—in obedience to the edict of a foreign emperor. There was no guest room for his parents when they arrived in Bethlehem, and his first visitors were shepherds, who also lived on the margins of society. In Matthew's account, Jesus is not only conceived by an unmarried woman but was also the descendant of women with dubious reputations. He and his parents become refugees in Egypt, fleeing a tyrannical ruler. He becomes a homeless preacher, without any place of his own; the people of his own town reject him, and he calls his followers to leave all and join him on the road. He befriends the outcast, heals the sick, touches the untouchable, feeds the hungry, and confronts the accepted religious establishment. His life of solidarity with, and action on behalf of, the rejected and deprived was consummated when he was rejected by the leaders of his people, handed over to the imperial occupiers, subjected to the death reserved for outcasts,

Following Jesus is a call to leave our comfort zones and to join him outside the city gates in the places of degradation and dispossession—whether they are physical, social, cultural, or religious—to embody the love of God for the excluded.

and symbolically excluded from Israel through crucifixion outside the city, alongside two criminals.

As the Wesleys rightly saw, following Jesus is a call to leave our comfort zones and to join him outside the city gates in the places of degradation and dispossession—whether they are physical, social, cultural, or religious—to embody the love of God for the excluded.

United Methodists on the Margins

The United Methodist Church's General Board of Church and Society has its offices in the Methodist Building on Capitol Hill, which is in Washington, DC, directly opposite the Supreme Court. This building symbolically locates The United Methodist Church in the center of political and state power with the intention of influencing the powerful for the sake of the excluded. This illustrates the paradox many Christians find themselves in. They want to change society but see that one way of doing this is to engage the powerful, and, if necessary, use the tools of the powerful. The General Board of Church and Society engages in various campaigns to lobby senators and members of Congress to persuade them to adopt particular policies or to reject particular pieces of legislation. It operates in a similar way with many secular lobbying groups. I am not criticizing the work of the General Board, but pointing out the complexity we face. Wesley also engaged the political processes of his day in his support of the campaign to end slavery. Not only did he write a devastating critique of slavery, he also encouraged Methodists to sign a petition to Parliament, calling for the ending of the slave trade. However, such engagement can never be for the pursuit of power and influence for the church. It must always be action motivated by the love of God, rooted in a life of solidarity with those on the margins. The church can engage faithfully in seeking to transform society only when it is willing to follow Christ outside the city gates. As Western societies become increasingly secular, churches will lose much of the social influence they have had. This ought not to be seen as a threat, but as a challenge to rediscover what it means to follow the crucified one—a new opportunity to engage in ministry with, for, and on behalf of those who are exploited, excluded, deprived, and rejected.

It is also important to note that speaking truth to power in national centers of politics and influence is not the only way we commit to solidarity with those on the margins. While big campaigns are important, it is no less important to stand with the poor, the victimized, the oppressed, and the marginalized in every community. Together, we can accomplish amazing things on a grand scale, but we can achieve much locally, as well.

Our General Board of Global Ministries equips, enables, and empowers The United Methodist Church in big and small ways to be a transformative force in the world for those in greatest need. Our United Methodist Committee on Relief is respected worldwide for its relief efforts, its educational impact, and its hands-on acts of mercy performed around the globe. From the Roma in Abony to the far reaches of Eurasia and the Czech Republic, from Africa to the Philippines, Mexico, and Puerto Rico, we respond in times of special need to those who are vulnerable in our midst. Day-to-day, The United Methodist Church is making a difference with the poor, the hungry, the homeless, the disabled, and those facing physical, mental, and emotional challenges. In our own communities, food pantries, thrift shops, feeding ministries, housing projects, and Volunteer in Missions projects abound. Each of these, and many more, is a way in which United Methodists strive to be a church that embodies God's love on the margins in every country and on every continent.

A Connectional Community

Connectionalism is the term used to describe the typical Methodist way of structuring the church. It takes somewhat different forms in different Methodist churches around the world, but it generally shares some common features. Chapter 3 described the structures of the church as the scaffolding that facilitates the building of the church, which is the community that embodies God's divine love. The shape of the scaffolding is important; it demonstrates how the community understands itself, and it gives direction to how the community grows and develops. While many of the specific features of connectionalism developed as pragmatic responses to specific missional and pastoral needs, the common features express key aspects of a United Methodist understanding of the church.

A Brief History of Connectionalism

The word *connexion* (to use the eighteenth-century spelling that is still used in British Methodism) was not originally a distinctively Methodist term. It was used to describe a group of people who were linked to, or united with, one another, and to the relationship that united them. When the eighteenth-century Christian revival broke out, the term was associated with the work of particular leaders, notably John Wesley, George Whitefield, Howell Harris, and Selina Hastings, the Countess of Huntingdon. Around each of these leaders developed groups of people who accepted their leadership. These groups were described as being in connection with the particular leader, so you had, for example, Mr. Wesley's connection and the Countess of Huntingdon's connection.

Early Methodism began as the group of people in connection with John Wesley; and because they were in connection with him, they were in connection with one another. The membership of the connection comprised three interrelated components: the ordinary members, the societies made up of classes and bands, and the traveling preachers. Over time, various factors emerged that united the people together. Perhaps the most important was Wesley's inauguration of an annual conference to discuss and plan the mission of the connection. Wesley saw this as an advisory body, with the final authority still being held by him. Out of the conference flowed basic rules concerning things such as the organization of the societies, the theology that was to be taught, the roles of the various leaders in the movement, and the standards of conduct expected of the preachers. To this was added collections of hymns, Wesley's sermons and other writings, common fund-raising, and a monthly magazine. These, together with the system of traveling preachers and Wesley's own preaching tours, created a deeply interconnected movement in a context where religious and political structures lacked coherence and strong central authority structures. In America, connectionalism developed in new ways as Methodism responded to the missional challenges of vast distances and the expanding frontier. In America and Britain, after Wesley's death, the conference became the focus of unity and authority. Connectionalism has continued to develop in response to new challenges.

Key Features of Connectionalism

Connectionalism is best understood as a complex set of interacting networks of mutual support, mutual responsibility, accountability through oversight/superintendency, and decision-making that are directed toward the promotion of scriptural holiness. Drawing on earlier discussions, we can state that this has three components: The first is integrated mission with holistic evange-lism at its center. The second is the provision of a context of mutual support and responsibility in which the members can grow in transforming love of God—or in traditional language, in grace and holiness. The third is the creation of communal life that embodies the divine love. There are a few other key features of connectional-ism that are important for our understanding of the church.

Itineracy—This is the practice where pastors are sent to a charge for a limited period of time to conduct ministry; they can then be moved to another charge. In The United Methodist Church, the appointment and sending of pastors is the task of the bishops. Other Methodist communions have different structures. Itineracy has its roots in the history of traveling preachers, assigned to particular areas to lead groups of local societies. There were diverse reasons for this practice, but chief among them was the creation of an order of preachers who served societies while maintaining a level of independence from them so that they could engage in innovative mission. This contrasted with the so-called "localized" preachers, who were resident in a particular congregation and often had other employment. In the contemporary context, much has changed, and most ordained elders have taken on the role of pastoring particular congregations, staying in one church, particularly when it is a larger congregation, for a considerable length of time. Ordained deacons often provide more "localized" ministry. There are often significant questions about the practicality of itineracy and the consistency of implementation in the modern Western world. This is not the place to address these issues. What is important is how we recover the spirit of mission that inspired the early traveling preachers, and how United Methodism can be structured best for mission, while recognizing that The United Methodist Church operates in diverse contexts.

Conference—The United Methodist Church has a complex, interrelated system of conferences. All ordained clergy are members of an annual conference, not of the local congregation or ministry setting they serve. Each local congregation (or, more correctly, charge) also sends lay members to yearly annual conference sessions. The annual conferences are the basic body of The United Methodist Church.[6] The annual conferences, in turn, elect clergy and lay delegates to jurisdictional/central and General Conferences, held every four years. This system of conferencing implies two important things about how we understand the church. The first is that, while the local congregation is an expression of the one body of Christ, it is only one part of a greater whole represented by the conference, which in turn represents the larger denomination. Yet the conference exists only as the network of local congregations and ordained clergy. Hence, while there is a place for local responsibility and decision-making with regard to the mission and the life of the church, there is also the need for overarching responsibility and decision-making. Another feature is the recognition that decision-making in the church ought to be the product of dialogue and discussion among laity and clergy together, in which the church together seeks to discern the leading of the Spirit. Unfortunately, in too many of our contemporary conferences, this has degenerated into political maneuvering and majority rule.

Superintendency—Connectionalism involves a network of relationships of accountability and superintendency. The ministry of superintendency promotes growth in holiness throughout the church, the supervision of pastoral and congregational ministry, and ensures commitment to the mission of the church. In The United Methodist Church, superintendency is an extension of the office of the bishop, comprised of a cabinet of district superintendents. Bishops have numerous tasks, but two are essential to the ministry of superintendency. The first is leadership in mission, expressed particularly but not exclusively in the sending of clergy to their particular charges. Bishops appoint clergy leadership to empower local churches, charges, and extension ministries to effectively fulfill the mission of making disciples of Jesus Christ for the transformation of the world. This is mission-critical work of incredible importance and impact. The second task is the distinctive function of general superintendency for the entire global church. United Methodist bishops are not part of a diocesan system; they are elected by their jurisdictional or central conferences and assigned an episcopal area. However, the Council of Bishops maintains a collegial general superintendency over the whole church. Hence, an important element of their calling is to facilitate the unity and mission of the whole church, not only the episcopal area over which they preside.

These are not the only aspects of connectionalism. Within The United Methodist Church, there are various general boards and agencies authorized to conduct specific tasks in furthering the mission of the church. There is the *Book of Discipline* that provides detailed regulations and polity for the life of the church. However, beyond the administrative and legalistic aspects of our denomination, historically, connectionalism served as a flexible, pragmatic, and innovative set of structures relating local communities of Methodists to one another in the service of mission, growth in holiness, and community building. Over time, many of these structures have become less effective, some are obsolete, and many have become rigid in ways that actually hinder the mission of the church. The major challenge before the church in our contemporary context is how we reinvent connectionalism in a way that draws on the best of our heritage but that motivates, empowers, and facilitates dynamic mission in diverse situations.

A Transnational Community

During the increasing tension between The Methodist Episcopal Church, founded in America in 1784, and the Methodist movement in Britain, John Wesley asserted that "the Methodists are one people in all the world."[7] While this might have been an unsuccessful attempt on Wesley's part to assert his authority over American Methodism, it was also a vision of unity for Methodism, a vision of an international connection that united people in different countries and different continents in one movement committed to spreading scriptural holiness across the globe. While unity is still elusive and controversial, Wesley's vision still lives as The United Methodist Church in transnational connection—with churches in the US, Europe, Asia, Africa, and the Philippines—does seek common ground. This section explores the significance of being a transnational church.

People's experiences of The United Methodist Church as a transnational, worldwide denomination vary considerably. For some in the US, it is largely experienced through mission trips and partnerships with congregations in other places around the globe. For others, it might not feature at all in their personal experience. In many places, being United Methodist is not as important as being "Christian," and awareness of our missional connectional witness is all but nonexistent. Many United Methodists have been involved in the struggles and debates over the inclusion and affirmation of LGBTQ persons (Lesbian, Gay, Bisexual, Transgender, Queer/Questioning) both within and beyond the United States. Each session of our General Conference challenges us to find faithful and creative ways to maintain unity and worldwide communion in the face of fundamental biblical, theological, moral, ethical, and cultural differences. For those of us outside the US, particularly for the small United Methodist churches in Europe, being part of a transnational denomination is an important aspect of our identity. For others, the challenge is staying connected to those who define the faith in radically different ways.

A Biblical Reflection: The Letter to the Colossians

Paul's letter to the Colossians provides an interesting perspective from which to think about the transnational character of the church. What is particularly interesting about this letter is the way it makes use of the language of Roman imperial propaganda, turning it upside down and applying it to the church. The irony of this is emphasized in that Paul is writing the letter from a Roman prison. In Roman propaganda, the Roman Empire, under the leadership of the emperors, had conquered barbaric enemies and established peace. Victorious generals were granted the privilege of a triumph, a military parade through the streets of Rome, displaying the treasures gained through the conquest and the defeated enemies. Through these victories, the empire was expanded to include conquered people in the sphere of Roman civilization, order, and peace.

In Colossians, Christ's work of bringing salvation is described as a victory over principalities and powers, leading to a public display of this triumph that results in cosmic reconciliation and peace. Unlike the imperial approach, this victory is not achieved through war and violent conquest but through a degrading death on a cross. The first fruit of the cosmic peace is found in the community of people who are united to one another by being united to Christ in his death and resurrection. It is a community in which "there is neither Greek nor Jew, circumcised nor uncircumcised, barbarian, Scythian, slave nor free, but Christ is all things and in all people" (Col 3:11). Roman propaganda portrayed the empire as a multinational society under the benevolent, civilizing rule of Rome. The identification of the crucified Christ as ruler over all powers and principalities undermines the empire's claim to benevolence.

The description of the church as including barbarians and Scythians provides a counter image of empire by including those who were regarded as the very opposite of civilization. Scythians were regarded as the most degraded of the barbarians. This radically diverse, multinational community is created, not through common allegiance to the Roman emperor, but to the one who was crucified by the Romans. Colossae was characterized by considerable ethnic and national diversity, but it is unlikely that this would have included Scythians. In all probability, the church did not have Scythian members. Paul is describing a vision of a transnational community that overcomes all the social, legal, ethnic, and traditional barriers characteristic of the Roman world. The congregation of Christians in Colossae is an expression of true transnational community, and, as such, should structure its communal life in a way that reflects this.

The term *transnational* is more accurate than international or global. Its significance resides in the church composed of people from many different nations around the globe, but with unity— across all difference, disagreement, prejudice, or dispute—as the greatest goal and the highest priority. The church is a new reality, created through the death and resurrection of Christ, which surpasses, or transcends, the divisions created by national and

> ## The church is a new reality, created through the death and resurrection of Christ, which surpasses, or transcends, the divisions created by national and ethnic identity.

ethnic identity. The church is the representative of a new nation, a new society in the midst of the diverse nations of the world, called to embody and proclaim the values and ethos of its ruler, the crucified Christ. Again the vision emerges, by God's grace and the power of the Holy Spirit, we are made one with Christ, one with each other, and one in ministry to all the world.

Being a Transnational Community Today

We live in very different circumstances today from first-century Colossae or eighteenth-century Britain. Yet we are called to be an expression of the transnational community of the Christian church. The contemporary world is in many ways caught in the tension between the forces of economic and financial globalization on the one hand and resurgent nationalism and even isolationism on the other.

We have become increasingly aware of how our lifestyles are part of a web of global transactions that have an impact on people in other parts of the world. Travel between major cities in the world may be accomplished in a day. Smartphone and satellite technology allow instantaneous communication with friends and acquaintances across continents. The smartphone itself was made in China for a Korean electronics firm with raw materials coming from Congo among other places. The number of phones purchased from a company will have an impact on its share price, which will bring wealth or loss of wealth to shareholders around the planet. As shareholders are not only individuals, but include large investment funds, gains and losses of wealth impact the pensions of people whose contributions have been invested in the funds. Our lives not only influence others, but are increasingly controlled by forces far beyond our control. Major companies move manufacturing plants to places where they can earn the most profit, locate their businesses in places where they have to pay the least taxes, and move money around the globe for their own benefit. Jobs are no longer secure. International crime and terrorism threaten our security. We are one world, a global community, a social network—whether we choose it or not. No action, no behavior, no message is personal and private anymore, and all actions have consequences. The church has a great opportunity to influence our planet for good.

Migration has become a major aspect of our globalized societies. Of course, migration is nothing new; I am a South African of predominantly European descent. The earliest of my European ancestors arrived in what is now Cape Town in 1652. At least one other family member was brought to Cape Town as a slave from India. Now I am married to a German and living in Switzerland. Today, migration is intensified. Highly trained and paid workers move around the world for short or long periods of time. Many others flee war, terror, political tyranny, economic deprivation, or environmental destruction. They are looking for new homes where they can live in safety and provide for themselves and their families. There are short-term migrant laborers who leave their homes to work in foreign countries to provide for their families by doing the dangerous, degrading, and dirty work the citizens of the host countries do not want to do. In Europe, we have new United Methodist congregations made up of migrants from Africa, Latin America, the Middle East, and Asia. Ministry to migrants has become a source of renewal for small United Methodist congregations.

Global migration and rising numbers of refugees and displaced persons are resulting in a backlash in many parts of the world. There is a renewed emphasis on national identity, interests, and security. In some cases, this has led to explicit and implicit xenophobia. Foreigners are stereotyped, denigrated, and sometimes abused and executed.

Being part of a transnational community in the intersection of globalization and nationalism places unique challenges upon us as a church; however, there is a positive dimension I would like to emphasize. Globalization, migration, and transnationalism provide us with a wonderful opportunity to learn from one another. For too long, the relationship of the more prosperous in our world with those less fortunate has taken the form of charity, welfare, rescue, and sporadic mission trips. While these have value, they perpetuate barriers dividing "us" from "them." Truly partnering with others in ministry who are very different from ourselves cannot help but lead to change. To truly know those with whom we serve is the key to lasting transformation.

To name a few situations: What can be learned from the churches in Eastern and Central Europe and their experience of ministry with and for Roma people, responding to centuries of discrimination and exclusion? What can be learned from Zimbabwean Methodists about embodying divine love in the context of economic chaos, dictatorial government, and political uncertainty? The United Methodist Church in Congo can teach us much about embodying love in the context of war and factional conflicts, where millions have been killed and wounded, and hundreds of thousands of women have been raped. The United Methodist Church in Russia and Ukraine is working out what *reconciliation* means in response to civil war in Ukraine and the annexation of Crimea. European Methodists are experiencing renewal as they engage in ministry with refugees and other migrants. The Liberian United Methodist Church has had to discover what it means to love others in the context of Ebola. In the United States, some voices call, and others resist the call, for a wall to be built along the Mexican border to prevent further illegal immigration. At the same time, a long-overdue effort of reconciliation with Native Americans is underway. Many other examples could be named; the point is that being part of a transnational community is a deeply enriching experience, if we open ourselves to it.

Being one church in multiple, different, complex sociocultural spaces and times also creates tensions and disagreements that challenge our ability to embody God's love, and it sometimes obscures our perceptions of what that love requires. What some regard as an imperative of divine unconditional love is perceived by others to be accommodation to culture. Being part of a transnational church provides a unique opportunity to listen to the critical and contradictory opinions of others as we seek together to discover what it means to embody the love of God. There is no simple or easy way to accomplish this. It is difficult, complex, and demanding, and it requires that we take up the cross of Christ and leave our own needs and demands behind. Our goal is to hear the voice of the other, and more importantly, to hear the voice of the Spirit of God in and through the voice of the other.

Conclusion

Bringing the three themes together, we can describe the church as a transnational, connectional network of communities, which, in diverse contexts, seeks to embody the cruciform love of God. One of the distinguishing features of this community is that it lives and ministers with and for people who are suffering, deprived, excluded, and exploited.

An honest appraisal of what it means to be a church for the margins—connected not only to those with whom we agree, but with those who interpret our faith in radically different ways than we do, and to expand this sense of community from the local to a worldwide, transnational perspective—can remind us of only one thing: this is God's church, not ours. Certainly we are invited to take part, not to be served, but to be transformed into servants of divine and sacrificial love. Church is generally so much bigger than any individual definition or description. It is well to adopt Jesus' prayer from the garden of Gethsemane, to humbly pray, not our will, but yours be done, O Lord. Human beings focus on what divides; God focuses on that which unites and builds up.

7

THE VISIBLE UNITY
OF THE CHURCH

When the early church summarized its faith in what has come to be called the Nicene Creed, it declared that we believe "in the one holy catholic and apostolic church." While the church proclaims its unity, this unity is often obscured by divisions and conflicts that result from diverse denominational and confessional structures. Each claims to be a valid expression of the one true church of Christ, some claiming to be more adequate expressions than others. Many do not recognize other confessions or denominations as genuine expressions of the one true church. There are divisions not only between different denominations or confessions but also within them. At times, deep divisions exist within single congregations. The history of The United Methodist Church, virtually from its beginning, has been one of tension, division, and conflict. Different theological positions have been represented by caucus groups that vigorously campaigned for their viewpoints. In some cases, those who disagree with a particular position have been not only criticized but also denigrated, and the authenticity of their Christian faith has been questioned. As I am writing this, The United Methodist Church is wrestling with how it can go forward as a united church given its deep division over the inclusion and affirmation of LGBTQ people in the church.

In response to these and other divisions, many Christians argue that unity is a characteristic of the invisible church, while disunity is the characteristic of visible churches. In the twentieth century, there was a significant movement to promote the visible unity of the church. United Methodists were vitally involved in this movement. In some parts of the world, it resulted in the establishment of united churches, while in others it led to greater levels of cooperation and common mission. The founding of The United Methodist Church in 1968 was part of the fruit of this movement. However, the unity of The United Methodist Church remains a goal we strive for rather than a description of the present state of the church. In this chapter, we will examine the significance of the unity of the church.

The Imperative of the Visible Unity of the Church

An obvious fact is that the Christian church is divided into numerous denominations. The Pew Research Center and other research organizations provide comprehensive statistics on many denominations, and these denominations are often divided themselves.[1] This division extends to the congregational level within many denominations, as well. Is the belief in the unity of the church a nonsensical concept? As we stated above, some have responded to the obvious contradiction by proposing that the unity of the church is an attribute of the invisible universal church, while the visible church is inherently divided into different conflicted denominations and churches. Christians who affirm their spiritual unity with all other Christians may cooperate as much as they like, but they should not expect to see movement toward greater organizational and institutional unity. By this reckoning, divisions within denominations over a variety of theological or ethical issues are no great tragedy. The organizational unity of a particular denomination has no deep theological significance.

A Biblical Reflection

As we discussed in chapter 4, the question of Jews and Gentiles eating together was a recurring issue in the New Testament. The barrier to sharing a common meal arose out of two issues. The first was that the Jewish kosher laws prevented Jews from eating common Gentile foods. The second was that of meat offered to idols. In the ancient world, most meat sold in the market had been originally slaughtered within a temple as part of a sacrificial ceremony. Christians were divided as to whether meat bought in the market could be eaten, particularly as one could not be sure whether the meat came from a temple. The significance of these debates in the early church is striking. Eating together was a visible, bodily, and public expression of unity. The New Testament writers did not propose that, because everyone was spiritually united, eating together was of no major importance. On the contrary, they made various proposals as to how the obstacles to common eating could be overcome. Part of the theology that underlies this can be seen in the letter to the Ephesians:

So remember that once you were Gentiles by physical descent, who were called "uncircumcised" by Jews who are physically circumcised. At that time you were without Christ. You were aliens rather than citizens of Israel, and strangers to the covenants of God's promise. In this world you had no hope and no God. But now, thanks to Christ Jesus, you who once were so far away have been brought near by the blood of Christ.

Christ is our peace. He made both Jews and Gentiles into one group. With his body, he broke down the barrier of hatred that divided us. He canceled the detailed rules of the Law so that he could create one new person out of the two groups, making peace. He reconciled them both as one body to God by the cross, which ended the hostility to God.

When he came, he announced the good news of peace to you who were far away from God and to those who were near. We both have access to the Father through Christ by the one Spirit. So now you are no longer strangers and aliens. Rather, you are fellow citizens with God's people, and you belong to God's household. As God's household, you are built on the foundation of the apostles and prophets with Christ Jesus himself as the cornerstone. The whole building is joined together in him, and it grows up into a temple that is dedicated to the Lord. Christ is building you into a place where God lives through the Spirit. (Eph 2:11-22)

From the perspective of first-century Jewish interpretation of the Old Testament, humanity was fundamentally divided into two groups: the people of Israel in covenant relationship with God, and the Gentiles who were not in covenant relationship with God. The covenant relationship was not merely personal but intrinsically communal. God's covenant created "a people." When

God in Christ draws Gentiles into relationship with God, this relationship creates a new united people. The hostility, the barrier that divided them has been broken down, peace between them has been established, and they have become fellow citizens. The statement, that they are no longer "strangers and aliens" but fellow citizens, is important. In the Old Testament, when non-Israelite foreigners were welcomed into the land, they were given special protection, as they were often vulnerable to exploitation. But they were still not part of the people of God. In the New Testament era, some Gentiles were attracted to worshiping one God and to many of the ethical values contained in Judaism. But they did not wish to go the whole way of converting to Judaism, which would have meant that males would have to be circumcised, the kosher food rules would need to be kept, and other ritual laws would have to be obeyed. Such people were the contemporary equivalent of the Old Testament "aliens and strangers." They worshiped God but did not follow all the detailed laws for the people of Israel. This kind of internal division is explicitly ruled out by this passage. There is one people of God created through the cross, and there can be no internal divisions. Theological unity was required to be embodied in practices that made it visible. Hence, common meals were of paramount theological significance.

A Wesleyan Perspective

As I argued in chapter 3, for Wesley, the core meaning of the church is "a congregation, or body of people united together in the service of God."[2] God established this body because "He saw it was 'not good for men to be alone,' . . . but that the whole body of his children should be 'knit together, and strengthened, by that which every joint supplieth.' "[3] They are "united by all kind of fellowship."[4]

> **The church is the community that embodies divine love when its members have a reciprocal love for and delight in one another. The visible unity of the church exemplifies what it means to be the church.**

The essence of true church is to be a community that unites diverse people together. A separated or divided community makes a mockery of these assertions, which are rooted in Wesley's theology of love. The church is the community that embodies God's love. In his sermon "On Pleasing All Men," Wesley wrote about love:

> Let it pant in your heart; let it sparkle in your eyes, let it shine on all your actions. Whenever you open your lips, let it be with love; and let there be in your tongue the law of kindness. Your word will then distill as the rain, and as the dew upon the tender herb.[5]

Wesley thought that love among Christians ought to have a greater depth due to their common union with Christ. This intensity arises out of two important factors. First, Christians have been transformed by God so that they may love God and others; hence the love among Christians is a reciprocal love that ought to cultivate a greater depth of mutual love. Second, Wesley argued that love between people closely united to one another involves a mutual delight. The church is the community that embodies divine love when its members have a reciprocal love for and delight in one another. The visible unity of the church exemplifies what it means to be the church. While some Christians contrast the unity of the church with its holiness, and then give priority to holiness as a way of justifying division within the church, this is impossible from a Wesleyan perspective; for Wesley, love is the essence of holiness. Thus the unity and the holiness of church are inseparably united. This makes separation, in Wesley's thinking, both extremely serious and desperately tragic, as it is a betrayal of the identity of the church. As he writes in his sermon "On Schism":

> To separate ourselves from a body of living Christians with whom we were before united, is a grievous breach of the law of love. It is the nature of love to unite us together; and the greater the love, the stricter the union. And while this continues in its strength, nothing can divide those whom love has united. It is only when our love grows cold, that we can think of separating from our brethren....The pretences for separation may be innumerable, but want of love is always the real cause; otherwise they would still hold the unity of the Spirit in the bond of peace. It is therefore contrary to all those commands of God, wherein brotherly love is enjoined.[6]

While Christians give a variety of reasons why they must separate from each other—theological disagreement, the corruption of

For Wesley, love is the essence of holiness. Thus the unity and the holiness of church are inseparably united.

the church, failure of leadership, and many others—Wesley was convinced that, at its root, it is always the failure of love. This might seem very simplistic, but only if we fail to understand the scope of Wesley's thinking. The deep commitment to the holistic, and therefore spiritual, well-being of our fellow Christians ought to be expressed in two ways. First, when we genuinely love others, we will respect their freedom of conscience; that is, we recognize the integrity of their commitment to follow what they are convinced before God is true and right. We would not condemn or pressure them to act against their conscience. If we recognize others as siblings in Christ genuinely seeking the will and truth of God, then we need to create in our churches structures that enable them to remain part of the community, even when we disagree with them. Second, if we are convinced that a person who is a sibling in Christ holds to theological positions or engages in practices in good conscience, but we are convinced that such positions and practices are detrimental to their spiritual well-being, we have a duty in love to remain in community with them to lovingly enable them to see the danger of their beliefs and practices.

Where we recognize that the people with whom we disagree are sisters and brothers in Christ, who love God and their neighbors and seek to live as faithful Christians, then there is a theological imperative to maintain a visible institutional engagement with them.

Visible Unity Is a Missional Imperative

Visible unity in the church is not only integral to the identity of the church as the community that embodies God's divine love; it is also integral to the mission of the church in the world. In chapter 1, I argued that, for Wesley, God's mission in the world is to transform human persons, communities, and societies so that they become permeated by divine love. The church is the central agent of this transformation through its words, its deeds, and through the witness of its own life. The latter is of crucial significance for, as I argued in chapter 4, it is not that the church *has* a mission, the church *is* the mission—God's mission in the world. The visible church is where divine love is taking form in the world, and it is called to be a demonstration in a world characterized by discord and conflicts. Its unity in contrast to worldly divisions and strife is a sign of the reality of God's love and an integral component of its mission in the world. As Jesus prayed, "I pray they will be one, Father, just as you are in me and I am in you. I pray that they also will be in us, so that the world will believe that you sent me" (John 17:21). People are drawn to Christ by observing the demonstration of God's love in the church, for they see in it the reality of the transformation. In an age of growing secularization in North America and Western Europe, the visible embodiment of love in the life of the church most clearly demonstrates the credibility of the gospel.

Negatively, the church's proclamation of the love of God rings hollow when its life is characterized by divisions, conflicts, and separation. All our talk about God has no meaning unless it is visibly demonstrated through our actions. As Wesley noted in his sermon "The Lord Our Righteousness":

> "How shameful and how countless are the conflicts that have arisen over religion! ... Religious conflicts also appear among the children of God; ... In all eras, very many Christians have turned their weapons against each other, instead of joining together against the common enemy. These Christians have not only dissipated their precious time, but

they have wounded each other's spirits, weakened each other's hands, and severely hindered the great work of their common Master! Many fragile people have been wounded by these religious controversies. How many of the "lame have been put out of joint!" How many sinners confirmed in their disregard of all religion and in their contempt of those that profess it! And how many of "the holy ones in the land" have been constrained to "weep in secret places!"[7]

Disunity and conflict within the church destroys the witness of the church to God's transforming love. Emphasis on the visible unity of the church raises significant issues in relation to the obvious diversity of the church.

Diversity: A Means of Grace

It is easy to talk about the unity of the church in theory, but the reality is that Christians have very different theological and ethical convictions. They disagree about how the church should be structured, about how Scripture should be interpreted, about how we should worship, and numerous other issues. While we will deal with some of these issues in more detail in the next chapter, the point I wish to make here is that a lot depends on how we approach the issue of diversity. Is it a threat? Is it a challenge? Or is it, as I will argue here, a blessing? I am convinced that theological disagreement and conflicting worldviews can be a means through which we can grow in love. It can be, in Wesley's terms, a means of grace.

In his pamphlet "The Character of a Methodist,"[8] Wesley refused to define the distinguishing marks of Methodism apart from theological points held in common by most Protestants of his time. He argued that the identity of Methodism was constituted by the character of Methodists who had been transformed by the grace of God so that they loved God and neighbor. Methodism is, at its core, a movement that embodies and proclaims the radical transforming grace of God, which overcomes the power of sin and enables us to love God and neighbor. If this is the core of our identity as Methodists, then the question becomes: How do theological and ethical diversity relate to the core?

Wesley explained this. He argued that, when the love of God dominates a person's life, it gives rise to particular habitual and enduring character traits. He provided a detailed exposition of these in his sermons on the Beatitudes: they include long-suffering, humility, temperance, gentleness, meekness, fidelity, goodness, trust, justice, benevolence, self-denial, peace-making, and sincerity. While Wesley argued that these traits are the fruit of God's transforming grace, he also argued that they did not grow automatically. They had to be cultivated through the use of the means of grace. We explored the means of grace in chapter 3. In review and summary, we can say that the means of grace are a variety of practices in which we engage; these are responses to God's grace, and they are means that God graciously uses to transform our character. After describing the transformed character of a Christian in his exposition of the Beatitudes, Wesley turns to Jesus' images of salt and light to argue that genuine "religion" is always social religion. Wesley argued that we can develop loving habitual and enduring character traits only through dynamic interaction with other people—Christian and non-Christian—that gives us the opportunity to concretely express love toward them. As we express love toward others, God transforms our character so we become more loving. Different contexts will provide new and diverse opportunities for expressing love to others. Hence the process of sanctification never ends.

There are always new opportunities and challenges that provide for new embodiments of love of God and others. These diverse opportunities for concrete interaction with others are also a means of grace.

> *Participation in a theologically diverse community can become a means of grace when approached as an opportunity to express deep love for those with whom we disagree.*

Participating in a church or congregation that is characterized by theological and ethical diversity can be one way in which we can learn what it means to embody God's love to others. Wesley described this as a "catholic" (universal) love through which our characters can be transformed. It can thus be a means through which God transforms us so that we become more like Christ. This happens when we cultivate character traits such as humility, patience, teachability, tolerance, self-control, thinking of others as better than ourselves, trust, hope, mutual respect, and many more. Such transformation is not automatic. Wesley was well aware that theological disagreement often gave rise to bitterness, anger, pride, a spirit of denigration, suspicion, and other unholy, habitual, and enduring character traits. Participation in a theologically diverse community can become a means of grace when approached as an opportunity to express deep love for those with whom we disagree. When we strive to understand different interpretations of Scripture, when we refrain from judging the behaviors and attitudes of others, or when we agree to respect and listen to people who believe very different things than we do, we create an environment where love might prevail. We follow Wesley's basic rules to do no harm, while doing all the good we can.

Being an active member of a church characterized by theological and ethical diversity and debate can be a means for becoming more holy. In fact, it provides a unique environment for growing in love for our fellow Christians that we would not have if we all agreed with one another. Hence, a theologically diverse community is not a threat to holiness, when holiness is understood as being transformed so our lives are permeated by love. Rather, it can become an expression of holiness to the extent that we actively use it as a means of growing in love for one another. Theological and ethical diversity is not good in itself. It is only of value when the goal of participating in such a community is growth in love. This does not mean that all theological and ethical perspectives must be incorporated in a particular denomination; some are clear violations of the divine love revealed in Christ. Nor does it mean that we should treat theological differences as of no importance. On the contrary, it is because theological viewpoints are important that we need to expose ourselves to alternative viewpoints and the criticism of others.

Centers and Boundaries

We have seen that understanding diversity as a means of grace does not mean that all theological and ethical viewpoints are acceptable. Over the centuries, churches have described what they hold to be the core theological and ethical positions to be taught in their churches. Some churches require people to agree to a statement of doctrine, and, in some cases, a statement of ethics, in order to become a member. As we noted above, Wesley did not think that the distinctive features of Methodism were best described in a doctrinal statement. That is not to say that doctrine was not important for him.

Perspectives from Early Methodism

Issues of doctrine, polity, and "right belief" are often described as a question of the boundaries of the church. Boundaries clearly separate those who are in from those who are out, those who belong from those who do not. Wesley's practice and theology suggest an alternative approach. Early Methodism had, as we have noted before, a very open membership requirement. All who were seeking a transforming relationship with God were welcome to become Methodists, but they had to demonstrate the sincerity of their commitment by living a lifestyle that conformed to the General Rules. Wesley specifically rejected the idea that agreement on specific theological propositions or agreement on forms of worship was a requirement for membership. Remember that early Methodism was not a separate denomination, but a movement that drew its membership from people who were members of other churches. Even among those who served as preachers, there was great flexibility. First, it was agreed that no one should be required to believe or practice something that they were not convinced, before God, was the correct thing to believe or practice. Wesley insisted that no one should be required to go against his or her conscience. He took this a step further; he argued that no preachers should preach anything that was contrary to the doctrine contained in the first four volumes of his published sermons and his *Explanatory Notes upon the New Testament* (*Notes*). He did not go into detail to explain what was and was not part of this doctrine. He recognized that, in a number of cases, his views in the *Notes* and the sermons were open to correction; not everything contained in them was part of the authoritative doctrine. He was also happy to work with preachers who disagreed with aspects of the doctrine contained in the sermons and *Notes*, as long as they did not teach against them.

Wesley's approach suggests an alternative to dealing with differences of scriptural and theological interpretations. He refocused the issue from the boundaries—what's allowable—to the center—what's essential. What composes the center of the Christian faith upon which all can agree? When this is established, there is room for considerable diversity in interpreting the boundaries and their significance. Of fundamental importance for Wesley was the transforming work of God in the human person. God acts within a person to reorient him or her from being centered on self to being centered on God and directed toward the well-being of others. So when Wesley came to describe what was central, he focused on this transformation.

The Center Described Theologically

The God who is love, loves all human beings, and, through grace, God takes the initiative in transforming the human person. God's grace is the power of transformation enabling human beings to respond to God. However, God's grace does not determine the human response. Human beings can respond positively to God's grace, opening themselves up to the further working of God in their lives. They can, however, respond negatively by rejecting God's grace. Yet, because God is loving and free, God can and does interrupt the negative spiral of human rejection with new gracious invitations. God's grace thus initiates a dynamic personal interaction between God and the human person. Wesley typically referred to a number of key doctrines to describe this change. We will briefly look at five.

Original Sin: Wesley argued that God's gracious action within a person can be understood only within the context of original sin. While the doctrine of original sin has been interpreted and misinterpreted in a variety of ways, what is important is the core affirmation that human personhood is characterized by a dynamic that is radically turned in on itself, so that the self and its interests are the determining center of our lives.

Prevenient Grace: Wesley affirmed not only that all human beings were subject to original sin, but also that God's prevenient grace was present in all human beings. This grace provides initial liberation from the effect of sin, making people aware to some degree of God's intention that we love God and our neighbors, and enables us to respond to this awareness. Human beings are thus enabled by grace to make responsible decisions about their lives—an ability Wesley described as the faculty of *liberty*. In a particular way, God's prevenient grace accompanies God's revelation in Scripture and the proclamation of the gospel, calling and empowering people to come to faith.

Justification and Assurance: Prevenient grace opens a person to respond to God and the saving love of Jesus the Christ. God forgives, and through this ongoing work of grace, we are justified—through no acts or efforts of our own. While people may prepare themselves for justification through the practice of the means of grace, it is God alone, and not our good works, that makes this happen.

Justification comes through faith in Christ. Once people are justified by God, the Spirit of God assures them as individuals that they are loved by God, they are forgiven for their sin, and they have become children of God. Wesley recognized that an awareness of the assurance of the Spirit differed from person to person, but he held it to be an integral dimension of Christian experience.

New Birth: Justification is always accompanied by the new birth, whereby God, through the Holy Spirit, transforms the person, liberating her or him from the power of sin, re-centering the person on God, directing and enabling the individual to love their neighbors.

Sanctification: The new birth initiates the process of sanctification, which is growth in holiness. The core of holiness is love for God and other people; hence, sanctification is growth in love. Sanctification was, for Wesley, the renewal and transformation of the heart— the inner complex of human desires, attitudes, and attractions— reshaping a person's character. This inner transformation is expressed in the transformation of a person's outward behavior.

What about other doctrines—that Jesus was fully divine and fully human, that Jesus died and rose again, that there will be a final judgment when we will be required to give an account for our lives? Wesley did not deny these and other doctrines; in fact, he insisted on them. The transformation of the human person can be understood only in the light of the overarching story of who God is and what God does, as found in the Bible.

What Wesley insisted upon, however, was that the importance of a doctrine lay in its relationship with the center. The further one moved from this center, the more room there was for legitimate disagreement. For example, in Wesley's sermon, "On the Trinity," he stated that the doctrine of the Trinity—that God is three and God is one—is essential for understanding God and is at the heart of all vital religion. Whereas Wesley unequivocally stated many times that love is the central aspect of God's nature, he allows a great deal of room on how one might perceive and understand the workings of the Holy Trinity. It is essential that we agree on the Trinity, but not that we all understand it in exactly the same way. This reflects Wesley's catholic and ecumenical spirit.

It is also important to note that Wesley often drew distinctions between God's transformative work and our human explanations of it. People who affirm the transformative work of God will differ as to how to explain and interpret it, just as they do the Trinity. We must be careful to focus not on the explanations and interpretations, but on the reality that God transforms us.

The Transformation of the Human Person Described Ethically

The transformation of the human person liberates, empowers, and motivates people to love God and their neighbors. We have already explored this in some detail, but we note the following here:

First, moral laws set forth in biblical texts (the Law and the Prophets, the Sermon on the Mount, Paul's letters, and the Pastoral Epistles) sought to define and describe what love means in diverse human relationships and contexts.

Second, discernment of moral law requires more than simple reference to concrete biblical commands. Communities, societies, and families work out what these commandments mean in each context. In his General Rules, Wesley related the requirements of the moral law of eighteenth-century England, and included things not found in the Bible, such as the ban on drinking and trading in spirituous liquor—a substance that did not exist in biblical times, but that was an application of the command to love one's neighbor.

Third, not all ethical and moral issues and positions have equal importance. Wesley, for example, argued strongly that the Bible requires that Christians do not eat blood. However, he equally strongly argued that this was an area where Christians could disagree. Again, the importance of an issue lies in its relationship to the fundamental commands to love God and one's neighbors. For Wesley, rejection of eating blood was clearly of lesser significance than that of drinking spirituous liquor.

Fourth, Wesley recognized that Christians would disagree on what it means to love God and one's neighbor. The clearest example of this is seen in the way that Wesley evaluated Roman Catholicism. Like most Protestants of his time, Wesley believed that the veneration of the saints and Mary in Catholic worship was a form of idolatry and, thus, a violation of the command to love God. However, he not only recognized that there were Catholics who genuinely loved God but also saw some of them as major examples of holy living. Christians can genuinely love God and their neighbors and still disagree on what that means in practice.

Conclusion

This chapter argues that the visible unity of the church is of central importance for the identity and mission of the church. I would go a step further in the light of the final section.

If a life permeated by God's love is the evidence of a transformed Christian life, then visible unity and love are core elements of what it means to be the church. Unity does not exclude diversity, disagreement, or conflict. Rather, if we engage our diversity, our disagreements, and our conflicts from the perspective of the transforming love of God, they can become for us a means of grace.

8

CAN WE BE ONE COMMUNITY?

Talk of unity is easy, but the reality is much more difficult. One of the key problems is that our religious commitments, beliefs, and practices are expressions of the essence of who we are.

Disagreements quickly become very personal, because they reflect expressions of our deepest understanding of what we believe is ultimately real and true. We argue what we believe is right and wrong, good and evil, and what we "know" about God. It is difficult to treat such matters with indifference. This is most intense within the church when we fail to recognize that the church does not belong to us; it is God's church, and here God determines truth and error, right and wrong.

Is it possible to be part of the same church with people we believe have fundamentally false ideas about who God is, what God is doing, and how Jesus fits into the larger picture? What happens when what one person considers to be God's will is regarded by another as sin? These issues are not new; they have been part of the life of the church for centuries. Individual issues may change, but the basic problem remains the same. The task of this chapter is to look at some key concepts from John Wesley's theology that can help us as we seek to live together as a community with diverse and even contradictory viewpoints.

John Wesley and the Catholic Spirit

By the time Wesley began his ministry, religious conflicts had been a significant dynamic in English history for two centuries. After King Henry VIII's break with Rome, some monarchs were Catholic and attempted to restore England to the authority of Rome; others were Protestant and wanted to retain the Church of England as an independent Protestant church. Rulers on both sides persecuted those who disagreed with them. Furthermore, the Protestants disagreed among themselves, with some wanting a more radical reformation of the church. This all culminated in the English Civil War and the execution of Charles I in 1649. The English experiment with republican government did not last; the monarchy was restored, and Charles II became king. Pastors who refused to conform to the new order were thrown out of their jobs and homes. Both of Wesley's grandfathers lost their jobs and houses, and one was imprisoned for continuing to preach despite an official ban on preaching by people who were not Church of England priests. Wesley's parents joined the Church of England as young adults. By the time Wesley was a young man, violent persecution had ceased. Protestants who were not members of the Church of England were tolerated under certain conditions, but they were excluded from significant state offices and from the two universities (Oxford and Cambridge). Catholics were no longer persecuted, but they were not permitted to organize or engage in public worship; some were suspected of wanting to undermine the government and of supporting England's enemies.

Early Methodism was not a denomination, but a renewal movement focused on revitalizing the Church of England. However, it soon drew members from other Protestant denominations. The issue of theological disagreement confronted Methodists in three important ways. First, as Methodism included members of different denominations, the key theological and practical differences among these denominations were brought into the Methodist movement. Second, Methodism was only one of a number of revival movements, which shared much in common but also divided on significant theological issues. A question of major importance was how the different renewal movements could relate to one another. Third, the relationship between Methodism and the Church of England was a source of controversy.

On a more personal note, Wesley was profoundly influenced by people with whom he strongly disagreed. This is perhaps best illustrated by his relationship with Roman Catholicism. During his time as a student at Oxford, Wesley was deeply influenced in his understanding of holiness by the Roman Catholic writer Thomas à Kempis's *The Imitation of Christ*. Later, he published an abridged form of it and widely recommended it to his followers. He further portrayed à Kempis as a model of holiness.

In our modern ecumenical age, it is not unusual for a Protestant to read, be influenced by, and recommend works written by a Roman Catholic. For an eighteenth-century Protestant, it was anything but common and would have been widely considered unacceptable. In numerous writings, Wesley stringently criticized and rejected Roman Catholic theology and practice, attacking "popery" and the errors of the Church of Rome. There were many beliefs Wesley could not accept: the Catholic interpretation of justification, which he interpreted as justification by works; reverence for images, which he interpreted as idolatry; the veneration of Mary and the saints; and the fundamental Catholic understanding of the Mass. According to Wesley, Catholic theology included ideas that were not taught in Scripture and that sometimes controverted it; it ignored and obscured biblical passages that contradicted its teaching; and its attitude and actions toward Protestants violated God's requirements of justice, mercy, and truth. At his most caustic, Wesley held that the pope was an antichrist. For Wesley, Catholicism was an adulterated form of Christianity. While he labeled it "vile" and an abomination, Wesley also tried to find ways to bridge Protestant and Catholic beliefs, to create a truly ecumenical spirit. On July 18, 1749, Wesley penned a "Letter to a Roman Catholic," where he attempted to refute gross misperceptions about Protestantism and clarify differences in thought, as well as identify common ground.[1]

Evidence of his ecumenical spirit is found in Wesley's affirmation of the writings and lives of individual Catholic writers, such as à Kempis, who asserted that the Church of Rome was a branch of the true church and recognized significant theological commonalities between Catholics and Protestants. He even asserted that he would have no problem if Roman Catholics joined the Church of England, and more astoundingly, that he would be prepared to be a member of the Church of Rome as long as he was not forced to violate his conscience.

How could Wesley hold such strong views against Roman Catholic belief while extending an invitation to civility and common ground? Some have suggested that we can find, as it were, two Wesleys—an open, welcoming Wesley and an exclusive, bigoted Wesley. There is no simple answer, for as in many other aspects of his life, Wesley was a complex thinker.

The Catholic Spirit or Holiness in a Diverse Church

Wesley provides an outline of the theology that underlies this seeming contradiction in two sermons; "Catholic Spirit" and "A Caution against Bigotry."[2] The genius of Wesley's theology expounded in these sermons is an expression of his understanding of holiness. Holiness requires an integration of belief and action: deep commitment to what one holds to be true, clear rejection of what one believes to be erroneous, and a way of treating others who see things differently. For Wesley, a person could be in deep error of thought or practice and still be a good Christian and an example of holiness. Error in one aspect of the life of faith did not imply error in all aspects. For this reason, it was imperative to work together as much as possible in the same church community. Let us explore this in more detail.

In "Catholic Spirit," Wesley proposed that, while Christians agree that a deep reciprocal love ought to characterize their relationships with one another, this is often not true in practice. In Wesley's terminology, they do not "walk together,"[3] and what prevents them walking together is that they "do not think alike."[4] The problem is that they have different theological convictions, which lead to different practices. His sermon was primarily directed toward people who were members of different denominations but who were part of the revival movement. It proposed that, even if their differences in theological beliefs and practices divide them, this should not prevent them from having a deep love for one another.

The key to this is recognizing what Wesley calls "one heart."[5] What, then, is this one heart? It is the heart transformed by the

> **Because we are all responsible to God for what we think and how we live, we need to have deep convictions about who God is and what God is doing in the world.**

grace of God so that we love God and our neighbors. This does not mean differences in theological ideas, religious practices, or denominational structures are of no importance. On the contrary, Wesley argues that, because we are all responsible to God for what we think and how we live, we need to have deep convictions about who God is and what God is doing in the world, which lead to particular ways of living and worshiping. For members of particular congregations, these differences concerning deep convictions emerge as a natural and normal part of our experience of worship and Christian community.

What is interesting is that Wesley also argued that a distinguishing mark of Methodism—the movement connected with him—was that it embodied a "catholic" (universal) spirit.[6] All people, regardless of denominational affiliation, theological ideas, or religious practices, were welcome to become Methodists. This, of course, was in part because Methodism in Wesley's time was not a separate denomination but a renewal movement. Wesley's theology of holiness expounded in this sermon provides a way for people who deeply disagree to recognize one another as people who have been transformed by the grace of God and who can be committed to working together as much as possible, without violating one's conscience.

The sermon "A Caution against Bigotry" addresses a similar problem from a different angle. The text for this sermon is the story in Mark 9:38-40:

> John said to Jesus, "Teacher, we saw someone throwing demons out in your name, and we tried to stop him because he wasn't following us."

> Jesus replied, "Don't stop him. No one who does powerful acts in my name can quickly turn around and curse me. Whoever isn't against us is for us."

Wesley interpreted this as a question: should this person be accepted as one who has been received by God into a relationship with God? Wesley then examined what it means to cast out demons; he argued that it means a person is being used by God to bring about spiritual transformation in the lives of others. If God finds one acceptable, then we should not reject this person.

Then Wesley turned his attention to what it means that a person is not following us. Should we be bigoted against a person simply because he or she does not "follow us"? Wesley offers a variety of perspectives. First, Wesley proposes that "not following us" may mean simply not being part of our circle—not "one of us." Second, he conjectures that "not following" may mean the person is of a different party or allegiance. Third, "not following" could mean holding different theological convictions or beliefs. Fourth, "not following" might indicate engaging in different practices and rituals. Fifth, it could mean being of a different sect, church, or belief system. Any of these could be interpretations of "not following" Jesus and his teachings. None of these understandings gives us the right to reject another who is doing God's work in a way different from our own.[7]

Having identified those who are not with us, Wesley then expounded on what it means to forbid them. He argued that it means to, in any way, hinder or prevent them from doing the work that they are doing in drawing people to a transforming relationship with God in Christ. This might not be direct action; it includes numerous actions that discourage or limit people in their work, including how we speak of them to others. On the contrary, we must do all we can to support and encourage such people in their work.

While Wesley focuses on people belonging to different denominations, it is important to note that his prime example—forbidding people to cast out demons—is the stated opposition of members of the Church of England and its leadership to Wesley's lay preachers. In other words, this applies within particular denominations as well as between them. Later in his life, Wesley argued that the differences that led more radical Protestants, such as his grandfathers, to leave the Church of England were not of such a nature that they should have caused division. In his sermon "On Schism," he argued that the only legitimate ground for a person to leave a church community of which they are a member is when they are forced to do something that their conscience forbids them to do, or they are prevented from doing something that they are convinced is what God requires of them.[8] When this happens, the blame for causing the division lies with the authorities who prevent people from following their consciences. It is worth noting that early Methodist conferences made the decisions of the conference binding on a person only if the decision did not violate the person's conscience. Wesley sought to hinder divisions within Methodism by providing for freedom of conscience. From another perspective,

Wesley adopted a number of practices that violated the rules of the Church of England where he felt they hindered him from his calling to proclaim the gospel. A key example of this is that he regularly preached in the parishes of other priests without their permission—and sometimes when they had forbidden it. Church law required that one should preach in the parish of another only when one had the permission of the resident priest. When Wesley proclaimed that "the world is my parish," he was not announcing a vision for mission but rather his refusal to obey church law that violated his conscience.

Let us draw some conclusions from this in relation to life within a church or denomination today:

- The core of our unity with other Christians is not agreement on theology or practice, but the mutual recognition that God is transforming us so that we love God and our neighbors.
- The crucial test for the affirmation of a person's ministry is whether God is using it to transform people's lives, not whether we agree with their theology and practices.
- Theological beliefs are important and matter because they shape people's lives; therefore, we must hold and promote our beliefs with conviction.
- We must affirm people's freedom to believe and act in accordance with what they are deeply convinced is the truth and will of God, even if we strongly disagree with them.
- The life of a church or denomination ought to be structured so as to promote as much unity as possible, yet respect genuine differences of conscience.

Theological Roots

Wesley's understanding of the catholic spirit is deeply rooted in the central aspects of his theology. In this section, I explore some of these aspects.

The Justice of God and the Responsibility of Human Beings

Central to Wesley's theology is the conviction that God is just and always treats human beings with justice. It was for this reason that he strongly rejected the Calvinist idea that God predestined some people to have faith and to experience salvation but passed by or rejected others. This, to Wesley, was fundamentally unjust. When God offers salvation to human beings, it must be for all people. God will not condemn people for not doing things that were impossible for them to do. Therefore, God does not condemn people for not responding to the gospel if they have not heard it.

Aligned with the concept that God is a God of justice is the responsibility of all human beings to be accountable before God for the lives that they live. God does not expect us to do what we cannot do, but God does expect us to use the knowledge that we have according to the ability that we have, in relation to the circumstances in which we live. Wesley insisted that we must act according to our consciences. When we act against what we sincerely believe to be true, are compelled to act in such a way by force, or in some other way are coerced to do so, we violate our consciences. This makes it easier to go against what we believe to be right, and thus makes it easier to disobey God and become once more entangled in the self-centered life of sin.

We Are Embodied Creatures

Wesley emphasized the obvious fact that we are not spirits floating around, but embodied creatures. This means that all our knowledge comes through our bodies. The only access we have to the world is through our bodily organs. The data we receive from them is processed by our brains. Even if we have direct communication from God, it is still processed by our brains. Because our knowledge is dependent upon our bodies, it is limited by our bodies. We were brought up in a particular place, in the context of a specific culture; we were part of a certain education system, met a number of people, and were exposed to particular sources of information; and on and on. What is important to note is that different people will have different combinations of the above, leading to different perceptions of reality. The way our brain processes data is dependent on psychological, cultural, philosophical, and other factors. As a result of these bodily processes, all our knowledge is subject to limitations, mistakes, and distortions. When we read and interpret the Bible, the same factors are at work, so that all our theological understanding is subject to limitations, mistakes, and distortions. Wesley went further and argued that God's gracious transforming work does not change this, for we remain in these finite and fallen bodies. In fact, in some cases, it might increase the likelihood of error; for when we truly love others, we will be inclined to believe them and to hear them empathetically when they may be wrong.

Linking this to the first point, because we are responsible before God for our lives, we also have responsibility to seek the truth and live in accordance with it. As limited and embodied creatures, we will make mistakes. However, God is just and does not expect the impossible from us, but rather expects that we live in accordance with what we deeply and sincerely believe to be true. Because we are limited embodied creatures, we will disagree as to what is God's truth and purpose, even when we recognize that God is at work in one another's lives.

Sin, Properly So Called

This brings us to a core problem in dealing with diversity within the church: how should we respond to situations where what one person regards as sin, another regards as God's requirements? In Wesley's cultural context, as we have noted, a particular issue was how one evaluated Roman Catholic worship. For most Protestants, the veneration of Mary and the saints was a form of idolatry and a violation of the first two commandments. For Catholics, it was a legitimate element of their worship of God. What, for one, was sin, was serving God for the other. Both could not be ultimately right, yet both claimed to be. Wesley insisted that both groups should be true to their consciences. While both groups must be convinced of the correctness of their beliefs, they cannot be absolutely certain that they are right. There is always the possibility that they may be wrong.

Reflecting on this situation, Wesley drew an important distinction in the interpretation of what it means to sin. He defined *sin* as the willing violation of the known will of God. Wesley described this as "sin, properly so called." He distinguished this from "sin, improperly so called";[9] actions that are, from God's perspective, contrary to the will of God, but that we do believing that they are God's will. Because God is just, God holds us responsible only for sin, properly so called, and these sins need to be confessed and repented of. In Christ, God forgives sin, improperly so called, when we are not aware it is sin and, therefore, do not confess and repent of it. In Wesley's thinking, Christians should do business with Christians, and all business dealings should be honest, just, and fair. On occasion, a fair price would not be paid, or full value would not be recognized, but through ignorance rather than through intent. Such would be sin, improperly so called; no harm was meant or implied. However, to knowingly take advantage of another through manipulation or malice was sin, properly so called.

This does not mean that we can live as we like and ignore God's will. Rather, the opposite is true; we ought to sincerely seek to discover what the will of God is so that we may live in accordance with it. In our seeking out the will of God, the presence and involvement of those who disagree with us is important. Their perspectives are important challenges to our beliefs about the will of God; by listening to them and reevaluating our views, we can come to a fuller knowledge of God's will. We experience the greatest benefit when they listen to us and do the same. A diverse community provides a unique opportunity for mutual learning and growth in our knowledge of God's will.

> *In our seeking out the will of God, the presence and involvement of those who disagree with us is important.*

The Law of Love

Wesley speculated that before the fall, Adam had perfect knowledge of the will of God and how to apply it to his life. He was required by God to fully and completely obey the moral law of God. However, after the fall, all human knowledge was subject to mistakes, limitations, and distortions. It is now impossible for us to keep the moral law without mistakes, not because we do not want to, but because we are incapable of perfectly understanding the law. One does not have to agree with Wesley's speculative and literalistic interpretation of the Adam and Eve story to agree with his analysis of the human condition. God is just and, therefore, does not require an impossible, errorless keeping of the law. What God requires of us is that we keep the law of love—to act out of genuine love for God and our neighbors as we described in chapter 2. It is important to note that, for Wesley, *love* meant, not only that our motives must be correct, but that we must also pay close attention to the consequences of our actions. Actions that are well intended but are demonstrated to have deeply harmful results are contrary to the law of love.

Summary

This section has offered the most complex argument of the book. Let me draw some practical conclusions:

- Be humble. Recognize that your knowledge is subject to limitations, mistakes, and distortions.
- Acknowledge that your most deeply held beliefs might be wrong.
- We need people to disagree with us to help us discover where we are wrong.
- Respect people's sincere beliefs, and do not in any way coerce them to act contrary to their consciences.

- Continue in deep relationship with people with whom you strongly disagree, who are acting out of love for God and neighbor.
- People with contradictory opinions and practices can be active participants in the same institutional church, because, in Wesley's understanding, they are not sinning, properly so called.

A Biblical Reflection

In Rom 14, Paul discusses how Christians should deal with controversies:

> Welcome those who are weak in faith, but not for the purpose of quarreling over opinions. Some believe in eating anything, while the weak eat only vegetables. Those who eat must not despise those who abstain, and those who abstain must not pass judgment on those who eat; for God has welcomed them. Who are you to pass judgment on servants of another? It is before their own lord that they stand or fall. And they will be upheld, for the Lord is able to make them stand.

> Some judge one day to be better than another, while others judge all days to be alike. Let all be fully convinced in their own minds. Those who observe the day, observe it in honor of the Lord. Also those who eat, eat in honor of the Lord, since they give thanks to God; while those who abstain, abstain in honor of the Lord and give thanks to God. . . .

> Let us therefore no longer pass judgment on one another, but resolve instead never to put a stumbling block or hindrance in the way of another. I know and am persuaded in the Lord Jesus that nothing is unclean in itself; but it is unclean for

anyone who thinks it unclean. If your brother or sister is being injured by what you eat, you are no longer walking in love. Do not let what you eat cause the ruin of one for whom Christ died. So do not let your good be spoken of as evil. For the kingdom of God is not food and drink but righteousness and peace and joy in the Holy Spirit. The one who thus serves Christ is acceptable to God and has human approval. Let us then pursue what makes for peace and for mutual upbuilding. Do not, for the sake of food, destroy the work of God. Everything is indeed clean, but it is wrong for you to make others fall by what you eat; it is good not to eat meat or drink wine or do anything that makes your brother or sister stumble. The faith that you have, have as your own conviction before God. Blessed are those who have no reason to condemn themselves because of what they approve. But those who have doubts are condemned if they eat, because they do not act from faith; for whatever does not proceed from faith is sin. (Rom 14:1-6, 13-23 NRSV)

As described in the last chapter, sharing meals together was a major issue in the early church. For us, this might seem fairly trivial, but for the Jewish people of the first century, it was anything but trivial. The laws about clean and unclean food were clearly set out in the Old Testament Law, and the eating of meat that had been offered in a pagan temple amounted to idolatry. In the book of Daniel, the refusal of Daniel and his companions to eat the royal food is held up as the first example of their loyalty to God in a Gentile environment (Dan 1:8-17). When Judea was under Greek occupation in the second century BCE, the persecution of Jews who continued to circumcise their children and maintain the Jewish dietary laws sparked a successful revolt against the Greek rulers. What one ate was a matter of life and death. It thus became the primary expression of one's loyalty to God. Paul created a controversy in the early movement by claiming it does not matter anymore. It was as controversial for Jewish Christians as any major issue is for contemporary Christians. Paul was advocating something that clearly violated biblical commands and that the people of Israel had maintained in the face of persecution. Let us note a few points from Rom 14:

- Paul describes those who do not eat as weak in their faith. Yet not eating certain foods in the face of persecution had been the sign of deep and strong faith.
- Those who eat must not judge those who do not. Only God will judge, and the weak will pass God's evaluation.
- The motivation for the action—eating or not eating—is the crucial factor. Are people seeking to honor God in what they are doing?
- People must not destroy the faith of others over disputable things.
- What is important is righteousness, peace, and joy—not food. It should be noted that, for the Jewish Christians, the dietary laws would have been considered an essential part of righteousness.
- Regardless of one's eating practices, what is most important is serving Christ.
- People of different viewpoints and practices must seek peace and build one another up.
- The fundamental issue here is whether one is, in faith, convinced before God that one's views and practices are correct. A practice is sinful when one does it even though one doubts that it is God's will.

While Wesley gives a more detailed argument than Paul, one can see that his major points are to be found here. Wesley's more detailed argument is well grounded in other passages of Scripture.

Practical Fruits: Holy Conferencing

It is common in United Methodist contexts to speak of "holy conferencing" as one way we should approach difficult and controversial discussions. Before we explore what this means, take a few minutes to reflect on the ways you have observed Christians discuss controversial topics. This might be in a formal setting, such as a congregational meeting or an annual conference, or it might be in personal conversation or through social media. In your experience, are these good examples of Christians' love for one another?

What exactly does *holy conferencing* mean? John Wesley has some very specific instructions as to how we should relate to others when we disagree.

The starting point is a genuine love for the other person as a sibling in Christ. This results in:

- mutual recognition of the transforming work of God in the other's life;
- mutual recognition of God's work through the other;
- mutual respect for the sincerity of the other's convictions, even when there is profound disagreement;
- mutual respect for the other's freedom of conscience before God;
- mutual seeking of as much cooperation and visible unity as possible;
- mutual support for the other's ministry;

- mutual commitment to the holistic well-being of the other;
- mutual viewing of the other in the best possible light;
- conviction of the truth and correctness of one's own theological and ethical ideas and practices;
- commitment to the importance of the issues on which one disagrees;
- humility to recognize that one's views might be mistaken or incomplete; and
- rejection of all attempts to coerce or manipulate others to think or act in a way that is contrary to their deep convictions of right and wrong.

This approach describes disagreements characterized by justice, mercy, and truth.

Truth

It is often said that truth is the first casualty in war; unfortunately, it is often also the case in debates and controversies among Christians. People select the data that supports their arguments and ignore or distort that which supports the arguments of their opponents. While in some cases this is done deliberately, often we do it without realizing it; our commitment to our own position blinds us to the weaknesses in our argument and the strengths in our opponents'.

Debates on disputed issues that are characterized by truthfulness require a careful and honest evaluation of the arguments and evidence that support one's own position, as well as those that support the positions of those with whom we disagree. The temptation to twist information so that it suits our purposes must be resisted. In evaluating the truth and validity of a particular theological and ethical position, it is always easier to see the problems and biases in the arguments of others. We are quick to accuse others of distorting the truth, but we should apply greater rigor to the honest evaluation of our own arguments.

There is a second dimension to this: Because of the limitations of our knowledge, our particular commitments, our experience of life, and our own deeply entrenched presuppositions, we sometimes misinterpret or misunderstand data and arguments without intending to deceive others. This is precisely where we need the help of those who come from dissimilar backgrounds, who have other experiences of life, and who approach the issue from a different perspective. By listening to their critique of our position, we can better evaluate the truth of the positions for which we argue. If we believe that truth is significant, then, to discern the truth, we need the opinions of those with whom we disagree.

> *A concern for truth is not merely about data and arguments; it is also about personal integrity and honesty.*

A concern for truth is not merely about data and arguments; it is also about personal integrity and honesty. In our debates and discussions with other Christians, we need to reject all forms of devious, manipulative, and underhanded methods. The point is not to win the argument at all costs, but to discern the truth in the service of love.

Mercy

Mercy requires that we treat those who disagree with us with a generous spirit that interprets their statements and views in the best possible light. It respects our opponents' intentions and ascribes the best possible motives for the positions that they hold. It rejects all attribution of hidden agendas, wrong motives, dishonesty, or manipulative intentions. Wesley proposed that, because we know our own sinfulness, we should always subject ourselves and our motives to the harshest judgment; and because we love those who disagree with us, we should view them in the best possible light, defending them against accusations of false motives and finding the best interpretations of their words and actions. We should reject the propensity to jump to conclusions, infer intent, attack, or insult those who oppose us. Even enemies deserve mercy, fairness, and justice in our quest for truth.

Justice

Justice requires that we treat those with whom we disagree and their arguments with fairness—doing to them as we would have them do to us. We must reject the use of selective quotations that ignore the context of a statement or claim, which leads us to draw different conclusions than the person we disagree with. We must affirm the strength of the arguments of our opponents and, where relevant, the weaknesses in our own case.

Justice must be applied to the way we treat not only arguments but also people. This means that we will respect the stated motives and intentions of people. We will focus on the arguments and not denigrate or in other ways attack the character or motives of the person with whom we disagree.

Summary

The goal of holy conferencing is that a community grows in love of God and neighbor. The point is not to win arguments, but to come to a more complete knowledge of God and God's purposes. The danger is that in our desire to advance what we believe to be right and true, we can end up sinning against God and our sisters and brothers.

Conclusion

Maintaining unity when there is strong disagreement is not easy. The drive to maintain unity does not ignore disagreement, but treats it as an opportunity. It requires sacrifice—that we take up our crosses in love and bear the burdens of creating community, in spite of disagreement.

Love motivates us to pursue unity in the midst of disagreement.

Humility enables us to see that we are not always right and others are not always wrong.

A community that is permeated by divine love will express this in the way it deals with and discusses issues of major disagreement.

In a polarized world, the church will bear witness to the transforming power of God when it demonstrates a way of living with contradictions and conflicts that manifests the love of God in unmistakable ways.

CONCLUSION

Embodying Love in a Broken Church

Our eight chapters have developed a vision of the church that has drawn on biblical texts, the writings of John Wesley, the history of Methodism, and the lived experiences of United Methodists around the world. In this conclusion, I want to look back at what has been discussed and then ask two questions. The first is: how does this match up to the reality of our congregational and denominational life? The second is: how can we begin to realize this vision in the lives of congregations and denominations?

The Journey So Far

In chapter 1, I sketched the big picture of God who is love and who has revealed what love is on the cross. Love is the foundation and goal of all of God's intentions and activity in this world. Human beings were created to reflect God's character of love and represent God's interests by embodying love to God and their fellow human beings. In doing this, they are a source of blessing to the world. Human beings have failed to do this and instead are characterized by a deep self-centeredness, but God refuses to give up on humanity and acts in grace to liberate human beings from self-centeredness. The transformation of individuals through God's love has as its consequence the transformation of societies and cultures, so that they express love through justice, mercy, and truth.

In chapter 2, I focused on the transformation of human persons by the grace of God so that their lives become permeated by divine love, expressed in the cruciform love of God and neighbor. This transformation is interactive, beginning with God's presence and action, which enables and calls for our response to what God is doing. A positive response leads to an intensification of God's transforming presence. The transformation involves a dynamic interaction of inner and outer changes. The inner change leads to a change in our way of life, and the change in our way of life reshapes our character. God's transforming action is a fundamental redirection of our lives that permeates all dimension of our existence.

In chapter 3, I described the place of the church in God's mission of love in the world. The universal, or invisible, church is made up of all people transformed by the Spirit of God. However, this universal church is manifest in the world in concrete communities of transformed people. These communities are distinguished from their surroundings in that they, in varying degrees, embody divine love in their communal life and in their interaction with society. The Holy Spirit uses active participation in such communities of people transformed by the Spirit to further transform us.

In chapters 4–6, we looked at various characteristics of the church that are rooted in the Methodist tradition, which shape the particular way that Methodist churches in general, and The United Methodist Church in particular, embody the love of God. The church is a covenantal community whose particular identity arises from its communal covenant relationship with the crucified Christ. This gives rise to it being a community that welcomes all into a transforming relationship with God. As a covenant and welcoming community, it is the embodiment of God's mission of love in the world. We noted that Methodism was a movement for sacramental renewal, which placed the celebration of Holy Communion at the center of Christian life; for it was here that the death of Christ was re-presented, drawing people into an increasingly transformative relationship with him. The way of life revealed at the cross stands in striking contrast to the dominant ways of life in human society. When Holy Communion is placed at the center of a community's life, it provides stimulus for becoming a countercultural community. Being a countercultural community places the community in a context of pressure and temptation to conform to the broader society. One of Methodism's significant responses to this was the development of structures of interpersonal accountability, providing support for its members who desire to continue to be transformed by divine love. Jesus was crucified outside the walls of Jerusalem between two thieves; being a community with the cross at its center means being a community with its center on the margins of society. Historically, Methodism was a movement that has thrived among marginalized and exploited people. I argued that contemporary Methodism needs to recover this identity as it seeks to do mission with and for those whom society excludes and exploits. Methodism has always been a connectional movement, with structures that link its diverse communities in a network of relationships of mutual support and accountability, directed toward mission. This gains a particular significance in The United Methodist Church because of its transnational character. As a transnational church, it embodies in a particular way the universal church, which is made up of Christians from diverse nations, cultures, and languages from around the world.

In chapters 7 and 8, I turned to the unity of the church and proposed that the visible unity of the church was not an optional extra but belongs to the core of the identity and mission of the church as the embodiment of divine love. The very real theological and ethical diversity in the church ought not to be viewed as a threat to the unity of the church, but rather as an opportunity to grow in love for those with whom we disagree. This diversity can be a means through which we manifest God's love in the world, which is so often torn by conflict. This does not mean that the church has no clear identity. The identity of the church is constituted by the central reality that God transforms human beings so that their lives become permeated by love for God and their fellows. It is this that provides the point of unity in a diverse church. The problem is that, for many people, theological and ethical disagreements are too intense to allow them to live in unity. In chapter 8, I showed how Wesley's concept of the catholic spirit enables us to affirm one another as siblings in Christ who are genuinely seeking to live faithful lives, even when we disagree with one another.

God's purpose is love, and God brought the church into being that it might embody and spread divine love. This is the vision for our church in a complex and broken world.

Is It Real?

This might seem like a great dream, but is it real? If your experience is anything like mine, this vision seems to be an irrelevant dream. Far too often, the church is not an embodiment of love; in fact it seems to be the very opposite. Church politics are often underhanded, devious, and nasty. Disagreements easily degenerate into vicious conflicts in which people seem to be in a competition to outdo one another in misrepresenting and demeaning others. Instead of being directed toward our mission in the world, far too often we are more concerned with our own comfort and security. I could go on.

However, the opposite is also true, as this book shows. There are many remarkable examples of church embodying divine love in our broken world, stories that cry out "God is at work here transforming people and communities!" In the midst of a broken world, we see God's reign of love breaking in, bringing transformation, healing, and reconciliation.

Continuing the Journey

The reality of the church is mixed, but that is nothing new. One of the striking features of the New Testament letters is how they describe the church in almost surreal terms—affirming it as the embodiment of reconciliation, the new humanity, the center of God's purpose—and, at the same time, describe with brutal honesty the failures and brokenness of the church. The treasure we have is always in earthen bowls. This recognition is the fundamental starting point to becoming something different. We receive God's justifying grace only when we recognize our unrighteousness.

We can open ourselves to the transforming power of God only as we realize our brokenness and failure. The starting point of our journey to a fuller realization of what it means to be the church is the recognition of our own reality and our dependence on the power of God. Recognition must then lead to two further actions: The first is *repentance*. In repentance, we confess our sinful contribution to the state of the church. We are part of the problem. The failure of the church is not the result of others who are in the wrong; it is because of us and our sin. It is the recognition that sin clings to our best motivated actions and words. The second is *lament*. Lament is identification with the church in its brokenness without ascribing blame. It is the deep awareness that, even with the best intentions, because of our human fallibility and finitude, we have contributed to the failure of the church.

Following repentance and lament there must be *thanksgiving*. Thanksgiving arises out of the recognition that, despite our failures and brokenness, God has been at work in amazing and unexpected ways. God has used transformed lives. God has used the church to bring healing, hope, reconciliation, and justice in our world. Out of this recognition we ought to turn to God in praise, affirming God's amazing grace. Thanksgiving leads us to recognize that God can transform us and the church to a renewed faith in the power of the Spirit. Repentance, lament, and thanksgiving give birth to a *new hope*, which motivates us to cry to God to pour out the Holy Spirit on the church to convict, transform, and renew it. This is God's work, and God alone can do it.

As Wesley emphasized, crying to and waiting for God to work are active tasks. We cry and wait by actively seeking God through engaging in all the means of grace that God has given to the church. We must be actively seeking the perfection of the church in the hope that God will meet us and transform us. So the next step on the journey is to renew our covenant with God and commit ourselves to working in God's power and in expectation of God's presence for the renewal of the church, that it might become a community pervaded by love.

NOTES

Chapter 1

1. John Wesley, Sermon 26, "The Law Established through Faith II" in *The Bicentennial Edition of the Works of John Wesley* [hereafter *Works*], gen. ed. Albert C. Outler (Nashville, Abingdon, various), 2:39.

2. John Wesley, *Explanatory Notes upon the New Testament*, vol. 2, new edition [hereafter *NT Notes 2*] (London: Thomas Chordeux, 1813), 1 John 4:8.

3. "A Collection of Hymns for the Use of the People Called Methodists," no. 136, *Works*, 7:251.

4. Sermon 146, "The One Thing Needful," *Works*, 4:355.

5. John Wesley, *Explanatory Notes upon the New Testament*, vol. 1, 11th edition [hereafter *NT Notes 1*] (London: John Mason, 1831), Luke 12:49.

6. *NT Notes 1*, John 3:36.

7. John Wesley, "Scriptural Christianity" in *John Wesley on Christian Beliefs: The Standard Sermons in Modern English*, vol. 1, ed. Kenneth Cain Kinghorn (Nashville: Abingdon, 2002), 87. The original can be found in *Works*, 1:170–171.

8. *NT Notes 2*, Rev 3:15.

9. John Wesley, "The New Creation," *Works*, 2:510.

Chapter 2

1. John Wesley, *A Plain Account of Christian Perfection*, http://wesley
   .nnu.edu/john-wesley/a-plain-account-of-christian-perfection/,
   §10, accessed January 10, 2018.
2. Ibid.
3. John Wesley, "On Love," §2; http://wesley.nnu.edu/john-wesley
   /the-sermons-of-john-wesley-1872-edition/sermon-139-on-love/,
   accessed January 10, 2018.
4. Ibid.
5. "Letter to the Reverend Dr. Conyers Middleton" in John Wesley,
   The Works of John Wesley, ed. Thomas Jackson [hereafter *Works*
   (Jackson)], 10:69.
6. John Wesley, "The Means of Grace" in *John Wesley on Christian
   Beliefs: The Standard Sermons in Modern English*, vol. 1, ed.
   Kenneth Cain Kinghorn (Nashville: Abingdon, 2002), 270. The
   original can be found in *Works*, 1:381.

Chapter 3

1. Sermon 74, "Of the Church" in *Works* (Jackson), 3:46.
2. Ibid.
3. Ibid., §5.
4. Sermon 92, "On Zeal" in *Works* (Jackson), 3:318.
5. *NT Notes 1*, Acts 5:11.
6. "Service of Word and Table I," *The United Methodist Book of
   Worship* (Nashville: The United Methodist Publishing House,
   1992), 38.
7. "Article XIII—Of the Church," *The Book of Discipline of The United
   Methodist Church 2016* [hereafter *Discipline* (2016)] (Nashville: The
   United Methodist Publishing House, 2016), ¶104, 68.
8. Sermon 74, "Of the Church" in *Works* (Jackson), §16.
9. "A Letter to the Rev Mr. Fleury" in *Works* (Jackson), 9:391.
10. "Article XIX. Of the Church," The Articles of Religion of the Church
    of England, http://anglicansonline.org/basics/thirty-nine_articles
    .html, accessed January 10, 2018, italics added.

11. See Article XIII—Of the Church, *Discipline* (2016), ¶104, 68.
12. Sermon 74, "On the Church" in *Works* (Jackson), 3:52.
13. "Primitive Christianity," *Works* (Jackson), 11:91.

Chapter 4

1. See the "Covenant Renewal Service" in *The United Methodist Book of Worship* (Nashville: The United Methodist Church, 1992), 288.
2. *NT Notes 1*, Acts 11:17.
3. *NT Notes 2*, 1 Corinthians 12:13.
4. Article IV. Inclusiveness of the Church, *Discipline* (2016), ¶4, 26.
5. "Minutes of Several Conversations between the Reverend Mr. John and Charles Wesley and Others," in *Works* (Jackson), 10:845.
6. "To His Majesty King George II" in *Works*, 26:105.
7. "Minutes of Several Conversations between the Reverend Mr. John and Charles Wesley and Others," in *Works* (Jackson), 10:855.
8. This is reputed to be Wesley's instructions to Thomas Coke when he left for America to establish what became The Methodist Episcopal Church. While it is unknown whether Wesley actually said this, he does speak of "offering people Christ" in other contexts.

Chapter 5

1. Harry Wiggett describes this in *A Time to Speak* (Cape Town: Pretext, 2007), 57. See also "He Shone with the Light of Christ" in *The Church Times* (December 13, 2013).
2. Wiggett, "He Shone with the Light of Christ."
3. www.umc.org/what-we-believe/the-general-rules-of-the -methodist-church. See also *Discipline* (2016), ¶104, 77–80.
4. See, for example, David Lowes Watson, *Covenant Discipleship: Christian Formation through Mutual Accountability* (Eugene, OR: Wipf and Stock, 2002); Kevin M. Watson, *The Class Meeting: Reclaiming a Forgotten (and Essential) Small Group Experience* (Franklin, TN: Seedbed, 2014); Kevin M. Watson and Scott T. Kisker, *The Band Meeting: Rediscovering Relational Discipleship in Transformational Community* (Franklin, TN: Seedbed, 2017).

Chapter 6

1. Journal entry March 2, 1739, in *Works*, 19:46.
2. www.umc.org/what-we-believe/the-general-rules-of-the
    -methodist-church, italics original.
3. John Wesley, "The Mystery of Iniquity" in *Works*, 2:462-63.
4. *The Unpublished Poetry of Charles Wesley* (Nashville: Kingswood,
    1990), vol. 2:404.
5. http://wesley.nnu.edu/john-wesley/the-letters-of-john-wesley
    /wesleys-letters-1776, accessed January 10, 2018.
6. See *Discipline* (2016), ¶33, p. 35.
7. John Wesley, "Letter to Ezekiel Cooper, February 1, 1791" in *The
    Letters of John Wesley*, vol. 8, ed. John Telford (London: Epworth,
    1931), 260.

Chapter 7

1. See, for example, http://www.pewforum.org/2011/12/19
    /global-christianity-movements-and-denominations/, accessed
    January 9, 2018.
2. Sermon 74, "Of the Church" in *Works* (Jackson), 3:46.
3. Sermon 92, "On Zeal" in *Works* (Jackson), 3:318.
4. *NT Notes 2*, Acts 5:11.
5. Sermon 100, "On Pleasing All Men" in *Works* (Jackson), 3:
    422–423.
6. Sermon 75, "On Schism," in *Works* (Jackson), 3:64–65.
7. John Wesley, "The Lord Our Righteousness" in *John Wesley on
    Christian Beliefs: The Standard Sermons in Modern English*,
    vol. 1, ed. Kenneth Cain Kinghorn (Nashville: Abingdon, 2002),
    2328–2329. The original can be found in *Works*, 1:449.
8. "The Character of a Methodist" is available at http://www
    .umcmission.org/Find-Resources/John-Wesley-Sermons/The
    -Wesleys-and-Their-Times/The-Character-of-a-Methodist.

Chapter 8

1. John Wesley, "Letter to a Roman Catholic" can be read in full in *The
    Works of John Wesley* (Salem, OH: Schmul, 1978), 80–86.

2. Sermon 39, "Catholic Spirit," http://wesley.nnu.edu/john-wesley/the-sermons-of-john-wesley-1872-edition/sermon-39-catholic-spirit/; Sermon 38, "A Caution aganst Bigotry," http://wesley.nnu.edu/john-wesley/the-sermons-of-john-wesley-1872-edition/sermon-38-a-caution-against-bigotry/.

3. "Catholic Spirit," §1, ¶10.

4. John Wesley, "July 9, 1766" in *The Letters of the Rev. John Wesley*, ed. John Telford (London: Epworth Press, 1960), 21.

5. "Catholic Spirit," ¶4.

6. Ibid., §3.

7. Sermon 38, "A Caution against Bigotry," see §2.

8. Sermon 75, "On Schism," in *Works* (Jackson), 3:64–65.

9. See "A Plain Account of Christian Perfection," §19.

ACKNOWLEDGMENTS

Writing is never a solitary occupation. Many people have in various ways contributed to this book. As a book on the church, it has been shaped by my own experience of the life of the church in diverse denominations and contexts. So I would like to thank the members and leadership of the congregations of which I have been a part. In particular the United Methodist Church in Kleinbasel, Switzerland, where I am presently a member; the Basler Münster congregation of the Protestant Reformed Church of the City Basel where my wife is the pastor; Stellenberg Chapel, Pinelands, South Africa, where I grew up and whose life decisively shaped my faith; the Mtata Uniting Presbyterian Church of Southern Africa; and the United Methodist Church of Winterthur Switzerland. In different ways each of these congregations has shaped and continues to shape my vision of the church. As part of the program of the Methodist e-Academy, we require our final-year students to produce a missional plan for their congregation. This has given me insights into what it means to be a United Methodist Church in the contexts of Russia, Finland, Denmark, Bulgaria, Germany, Latvia, the Czech Republic, Serbia, Romania, Switzerland, and Hungary.

The idea for this book arose out of involvement in The United Methodist Church's Council of Bishops' Commission on a Way Forward. As we struggled together to find a way of structuring the church to accommodate people with contradictory theological perspectives, it became clear to me to me that far more important than the structural changes was the need for a common vision of the identity and mission of church. This book is my contribution to the process of building such a common vision. Working with United Methodists from very different contexts and with diverse theological perspectives has been a formative experience and contributed in many ways to this book. I wish to thank the members and moderators of the commission for providing a very stimulating context, which contributed to the development of the ideas presented in this book. That is not to say that they would all agree with all that I have written, but even when we disagree, I have learned from them.

The regular meetings of the commission and related work resulted in my being away from home on a regular basis over the past year. The strain on my family was intensified when I came up with the crazy idea of writing this book; I am deeply grateful to my wife, Caroline, and our sons, Carlo and Ernst, for their love, support, encouragement, and patience throughout this process. Also, a special word of thanks is due to our friend Ernst Geiger, who helped out when I was away ensuring that the family was fed and the dog got his regular exercise.

I am grateful to Brian Milford, president of The United Methodist Publishing House, for taking on the publication of the book, and to Susan Salley, Brian Sigmon, Sally Sharpe, Barbara Dick, and Dan Dick for their editorial work, and, in particular, for making my academic language into something suitable for all members of the church.